Meet the Buddha
Kill the Buddha

How To Awaken To Your Natural Joy

To Sheryl,
Good luck on the meditation.
Feel free to contact me if you need
any help. Peace & Joy.

by

Marshall Stern

Satyagraha

Publishing

Published by Satyagraha Publishing, Kissimmee, FL USA

ISBN: 978-0-9854652-6-1

Library of Congress Control Number:2013951112

Edited by Katie O'Sullivan

DEDICATION

I would like first of all to dedicate this book to a great teacher of mine who's name was Sid Arthur (really) Stern and who taught me many things without knowing he was teaching or that I was learning. Thank you Dad. And to my soul mate who taught me there was such a thing with her constant support and loving kindness. My Sweetie Pie, Nancy Howland Walker. And of course my two favorite skeptics, my wonderful son and daughter, Craig and Melody whom I love more than I could possibly express in words.

CONTENTS

FOREWORD

The Main Hall
Yen Tu Buddhist Zen Monastery,
late noon, December, 2013

"Excuse me, lady! Please, this place is for monks only," I said to a tall foreign woman who was in quite deep meditation on the chair I had just left to go beat the bell announcing time for Buddhists to bow the Buddha.

She slowly opened her eyes and smiled softly, with a very sincere attitude. Quickly, she moved to a place on the floor beside where she had been sitting and continued to meditate, while other foreign visitors were walking around to visit.

About ten minutes later, waiting for her meditation to finish, I stood in front of her.

"Where are you from?"
"I'm from Chicago, America."
"Oh! What is your name please?"
"Nancy!" She answered me politely.

I was quite surprised to see a western person who just sat to meditate in the main hall instead of walking around to visit and take photos as most do when they come here to Yen Tu Temple.

Since then we became friends through e-mails and Facebook. Nancy works on a Cruise ship that travels around Asia, and sometimes docks at Halong Bay, 50 km from our Yen Tu mountain.

Yen Tu is the most famous spot for Vietnamese Buddhists to make a pilgrimage. I invited Nancy to visit and she agreed.

And this is when I met Marshall, Nancy's husband, and my second surprise. We spent some hours together on Yen Tu mountain traveling and talking, often about Dharma. I was surprised to receive this book from Marshall as a special gift for me. When I looked at the book, I was even more surprised by its title *Meet the Buddha, Kill the Buddha*.

"Meet the Buddha, kill the Buddha" is a very popular saying for Zen practitioners. I was surprised about the title, as before I saw it on his book I thought this sentence only existed in Zen sects in China and Vietnam, NOT in the West. But here, Marshall took it for his Dharma expression in a very special way.

Marshall is the author of the Dharma book that you are reading. Before I received his book, though we had talked about Dharma, I didn't realize that he was such a "MASTER OF DHARMA." When I read this book I CAN FEEL its value throughout the experience of practicing Dharma. With enthusiasm, eager to share his knowledge and experience of the Dharma, Marshall describes systematically and scientifically all his knowledge about the Dharma, those ever proven throughout his life for spreading the Dharma.

For me, this is a very helpful document for beginners starting to study Buddhism. It provides most basic knowledge of the Dharma through Marshall's vivid expression. He has so many years of practicing the Dharma, and has had a treasure of experiences on the way forward to the Truth.

This is a very interesting, practical, and useful book for everyone who wants to read about the religious practice on the path of Truth that the Buddha taught. Through insight, Marshall's understanding (a master of Buddhism) and by grace you have been fortunate to find this book *Meet The Buddha, Kill The Buddha*!

Thich Truc Tu Thuan
Monk
Yen Tu Temple, Vietnam

PREFACE TO THE SECOND EDITION

I finished and printed the first copy of *Meet The Buddha Kill The Buddha* in October of 2013. I had begun writing it in July. That's a pretty fast turn around for a book from blank page to completed product, including all of the rewriting and editing. I was under a very hard deadline and really had no other choice than to work as quickly as I could. I am still very proud of the result, and have received thank you notes and great reader reviews as a result of sharing the book. However, I had always wanted to go back and rewrite the book with a more meditative approach, if only I could find the time.

This year, two weeks before I was to fly to Asia to begin another eight months of teaching, I had what is called a v-tach storm. That is when an internal defibrillator (which I have had since 2001) goes off in series successive shocks. In my case the device shocked me ten times in a one-hour period. Needless to say that was the end of my plans to go to Asia. As it turned out, after testing I was told that I was in need of a new heart. I had been dealing with heart disease for the past 31 years but up until now (with the exception of three prior bypass surgeries) I lived a fairly normal life.

Whatever comes to me in life has both good and bad elements and it is my strong intention to find the good and the opportunity in a challenging situation. The thought of a heart transplant was very frightening to confront, as it put me face to face with imminent mortality. Hard, but ultimately liberating. And part of the good was that now I had time to devote to certain projects.

The illness provided me the motivation and opportunity for much deeper meditation and reflection, and the time to use that better understanding to rewrite this book.

And that is how, dear reader, you now hold this second edition of *Meet The Buddha Kill The Buddha* in your hands. It includes Zen Stories that came to me in meditations. It is 12,000 words longer than the first edition, as I worked to be as clear as possible while explaining things more fully and including as much supporting information as I could.

Although I am still proud of the first edition, it is my belief that this second edition takes what was already a fine work and adds a golden sheen to it.

May this book help you to find and claim your Natural Joy.

Marshall Stern
Kissimmee, Florida
August, 2016

ACKNOWLEDGMENTS

Most importantly I want to acknowledge the unwavering support of my wife, Nancy, without whose help this would all still be cluttering up my mind instead of being cleaned and organized in the form of a book.

My children Craig and Melody who never let me get away with anything that can't be logically explained. I agree that belief is inferior to direct knowledge.

Kenjo Michael Aronoff who has been more a brother to me than a friend, with whom I have shared the spiritual journey for the past thirty years that led to this book.

Katie O'Sullivan for editing and making me sound like I can actually put two words together without hurting anyone. You make me look good and I still am willing to have your babies.

My dear friend Thic Truc Tu Thuan with whom I have had many Dharma discussions though he is in Vietnam and I in the U.S. thanks to Facebook messenger. Though there is a language barrier it has proven unequal to our ability to understand each other perfectly.

Finally to all of the listeners of Awakened America and students of Zenprov and Zen Buddhism 101 on Udemy.com, as well as the guests who attended my lectures on Celebrity Millennium and kept noodging me to write a book already! All I can say is, you asked for it.

Love and peace to you all.

INTRODUCTION

This book is an attempt to boil down to its essentials the fundamentals of Buddhism. At its heart, Buddhism is a very simple set of ideas. It is only because some practitioners like to make things sound soooo complicated- thereby raising their own stock as being soooo evolved and soooo intellectual because they understand it and you don't, (*breathe...*), that it gets complicated at all.

Seriously though, I appreciate everyone who has taken the time to write a book on Buddhism and I am sure they had the best of intentions when writing. These books are fine for experienced practitioners and even new and intermediate practitioners who have access to a teacher who can explain some of the more complicated ideas. This book was originally conceived as a simple straightforward introduction to Buddhism for those who have had little or no contact with it.

But as it turns out, this book is for experienced Buddhists as well. I have had lifelong Buddhists in Asia come up to me after reading my book or hearing me speak to tell me that this was the first time they understood what it was all about. This has happened on numerous occasions. But the main audience for whom this is written is for those who have no or very little contact with this ancient and phenomenal religion/ philosophy. I can actually sum it up in one simple sentence:

Buddhism is all about ending suffering. That's it. Full stop.

I could end the book right there but I would have a hard time justifying the fifteen bucks or so you have just paid to purchase it.

Honestly, I have never understood why people who teach Buddhism insist on couching everything in veiled mystical terms, thereby narrowing the audience for this very important information. I know when I started wanting to learn about Buddhism I had to be very careful about which books I chose, being cautious not to buy ones that either were too dense or were filled with Sanskrit and Pali words. Needless to say, there were a lot of those. Buddhism is very practical and very susceptible to the application of some good ol' common sense. It is also extremely accessible. There is no need to complicate it. It is very simple and easy to understand, if not easy to implement. That's where the work should come in when practicing Buddhism. Not in understanding the very simple and practical thought, but in applying these clear principles to your life.

The Buddha was very clear in one instance when asked about how the people should approach different doctrines and how they can tell which are true and which are not. The Buddha said - and I love this - that they should always apply whatever their own hearts and minds told them. He warned them not to rely on authorities or religious scripture or any outside source unless it complied with their own understanding of what is True. He also said to look at what the wise thought but ultimately it was up to each person to find the answers within themselves. What a cool thing for the founder of a religion to say.

The Truths contained within Buddhism are applicable to everyone. It is the world's oldest and most successful self-help program.

Do you ever suffer? Of course you do. Would you like to live your life without suffering? Of course you would. The answer to how one can achieve a joyful and wonderful life here and in this life is what Buddhism is all about.

What I have attempted to do in *Meet The Buddha, Kill The Buddha* is to set out as clearly and as simply as possible my personal understanding of Buddhist philosophy and how to apply it in your own life. It is my intention that this book becomes a practical help to you in your life. I mean, if you can't use knowledge to actually improve your life, why bother attaining it to begin with? That sounds too much like school.

Now why is the book entitled *Meet The Buddha, Kill The Buddha*? Because Buddhism is a very practical religion. Now think for a minute, what is the purpose of a religion? Is it to set you up with a collection of dogma and limit the scope of your thinking or is it to get you on the right path so that you can find your own Truth. And how do you know it's the right path? Because it feels better and lighter the further you walk it. So that is the reason the book is called *Meet The Buddha* at least. I am introducing you to the Buddha and Buddhist thought in order to give you some idea of the path the Buddha suggested you walk if you want to be free of suffering.

Why *Kill The Buddha*? I promise I will discuss this in detail in the last chapter of the book but until then let me give you a brief explanation.

The Buddha's teaching seeks to make him and this religion obsolete to adherents in their eventual evolution towards total liberation. In fact, it fills the role I believe all true religion should fill: it serves as a vehicle to deliver its adherents to freedom from dependence upon anything, including itself. Any religion or system of thought which frees you from everything but itself is not of much value in my book. And since this *is* my book, I get to say what is. (Ah, the power!!!)

Actually *Meet The Buddha, Kill The Buddha*, derives from a very well known koan (a term which refers to a paradox to be meditated upon) that states, "If you meet the Buddha on the road, kill him." The phrase is attributed to a ninth century Zen Buddhist Master named Lin Chi who was also the founder of the Rinzai sect of Zen and the creator of the idea of koans to begin with.

You might understandably and mistakenly think this quote comes from a source hostile to Buddhism. After all, it doesn't sound very reverent. It sounds kind of violent and disrespectful to the Buddha. But, "killing" in this case is just a metaphor for letting go. To find the Buddha you must look within. If you are on the road looking for him, you are looking in the wrong place. Whatever you find out there you may mistake for the Buddha, but the only true Buddha is to be found in your own heart and mind.

The Buddha said, "Do not mistake the finger pointing at the moon for the moon itself." Clearly the Buddha was concerned that followers would come to worship him, his words and life story, and miss the whole point of it. Certainly he would agree with the sentiment of killing the Buddha once you have met him, as long as it really was just metaphorical.

It might be better to say, "Learn from the Buddha, and then take what you have learned and become your own guru." It's just not a snappy title.

The goal of any parent, teacher, leader, or deity worth their salt should be to make themselves and their teaching obsolete. To act as a sort of runway, providing a level surface upon which the spirit can get a running start and take off, leaving the runway/teacher behind as it ascends to the heavens.

So come in and Meet the Buddha. Learn as much as you need to know and take full advantage of his wise and wonderful teaching. Use those things you find helpful and which serve to promote your deeper understanding and eventual liberation.

Then Kill the Buddha. When you have learned all you need to learn and are ready to go on, do not hesitate to leave all of it behind and fly away. Metaphorically Kill the Buddha.

Make nothing so sacred that it cannot be discarded. In the end there is only you, and it is there, without any aids or crutches, that you must stand in your own Buddha Nature to achieve full and final liberation.

ABOUT THE AUTHOR
(WHY ME?)

I have been a Zen Buddhist my whole life. I didn't know it my whole life, but I do now. From my earliest memories, I can recall looking for answers to questions usually too big to be a child's occupation. At a very young age I experienced the death of an adult in my bungalow colony (a co-op cluster of small rental summer homes.) She had choked on something and died. I was not present at this event, but was at home in my bungalow fast asleep. Nevertheless I woke up from my deep sleep and felt as though I could not breathe. I kept saying I couldn't catch my breath. I was about six years old when this happened and from that time forward I became very interested in understanding life and death.

I was raised in the Jewish faith in Flushing, Queens in New York, and attended Hebrew school (most of which time I spent being sent to the Rabbi's office) and High Holiday services along with my family (most of which time I spent exploring the secret and out-of-bounds nooks and crannies of the synagogue). Needless to say, other than getting in a good deal of trouble, my early experience with religion was not transformational, certainly not in a spiritual sense. After my Bar Mitzvah at age 13, I rarely if ever went to shul.

As I grew older, the urge to understand who I was and what life was all about grew stronger. I dropped out of high school, started taking drugs and did what many other people did in the 60's, taking Timothy Leary's admonition to heart. I turned on, tuned in and dropped out. Unfortunately, I was only 14 at the time, so these were not decisions supported by my parents. They insisted I either go back to school, (a fate worse than dull boring death as far as I was concerned) or enter a treatment program. When I balked, they threatened to put me in a residential program. That got my undivided attention. I entered a gestalt-therapy-encounter-group-based community that I attended four days a week for up to eight hours a day. The rules were: no drugs, no distractions, no unhealthy relationships and deal with your feelings. For the next two years I was immersed in this intense program of self-discovery. I was transformed in many ways.

As a result of this experience at a very young age (15-16,) I worked as an assistant helping to train Social Work students at Adelphi University.

Upon returning to high school, I found myself in a sort of teenage limbo. I was now fluent in the language of my inner emotions and ways of thinking. Because of that, I had a great deal of trouble relating to my fellow schoolmates who were still very into partying and being stupid adolescents. (Not really a bad thing, especially if you are a stupid adolescent and want to have fun.) Encountering your friends on a deep emotional level was not a great strategy for becoming popular in high school, and so my only friends were the ones I had gone through the program with. We had deep discussions and deep relationships. Anything less felt hollow to me.

When I began college, all of my friends chose different schools, and I was left basically alone. I fell in with a group of Meher Baba followers for a while, but dropped that when it turned out the "spiritual master" of our group was more interested in chasing tail than enlightenment. But during this period something happened to me that became pivotal and started me on a serious and concerted effort to find spiritual truth.

I was being driven home one night by one of the Baba followers. Let's call him Louie. Louie was an older guy (I was 18 at this point, so someone in their upper twenties appeared ancient to me) who had one incomplete to finish in order to get his Masters degree in Psychology. Instead, he was driving gypsy cabs and delivering pizza. He'd had this incomplete for several years, and showed no sign of doing anything about it. On this particular night, I asked him why he didn't just finish already. He responded by saying, "When G-d wants me to do it, I will do it."

Now, up until this point I had always dealt with these guys with a sarcastic sense of humor, but this night something different happened. I felt a deep sense of wrongness about what he said and it manifested in the form of righteous indignation. Rather than making a joke, which I would normally do, I yelled at him. "Don't blame G-d. What a crock of shit. There is no G-d!"

At that exact moment I felt something hit me in the middle of my forehead and I started to experience a vision. We were parked on 45th Avenue in Flushing facing west, and I can remember the lights of the street leading to Shea Stadium were all lit up for a night game. This scene in front of me started to melt before my eyes, and what was underneath was revealed to me - the Truth beneath the facade. All the buildings and the roads and the pavement melted away and revealed a beautiful garden. I understood this to mean that the original Garden is still there but we have paved over it. I thought about how there is always construction on the roads and how the pavement cracks as grass grows up through it. For me the message was that if we stop paving over it, we can live in paradise. I took this to be literal and metaphorical. It was a holistic experience that involved sight and sound, and most importantly my whole being understood everything in that moment. I saw how everything was connected and I felt that I had access to all knowledge simply by needing the information and understanding the principle that forms the foundation of the Universe.

For the next year and a half, I continually experienced visions of this type. It was amazing on one level, but very disconcerting on another very practical level. I saw deeply into the true nature of things, but found it even harder to interact with "normal" society, which seemed so shallow and paper thin to me. It left me feeling isolated from the world and everyone in it. I started feeling a profound sense of loneliness. I prayed to G-d one night to take this sight from me and let me have a normal life. The visions ceased.

The visions ceased, but that intimate feeling of being one with the Truth never left me entirely. I had seen the Truth and had knowledge that could not be erased. It was a spiritual case of "How You Gonna Keep 'em Down On The Farm After They've Seen Paree?" I had seen Paree, and the farm seemed awfully small and cramped to me now.

I spent the next twenty years or so investigating religions and spiritual traditions, trying to find in reality what I had seen in the visions. In every religion I tried, there was always the seed of Truth, but invariably I would find a place where the road diverged and ended up lost in a wilderness of dogma.

At first I joined the Meher Baba followers and though I loved Baba, as I mentioned before, I found the leader less than honorable. Next I remembered my father reading a book when I was small called *The Sleeping Prophet*. It was a biography of Edgar Cayce and the amazing "readings" he did while in an unconscious state. He was a Sunday school teacher and very religious, so it is not surprising that many of his readings are couched in Christian terms. I went to the bookstore and purchased a copy. This book had a profound impact on me and got me in touch with how much I longed for a connection with G-d. I joined Cayce's foundation, The Association for Research and Enlightenment and attended weekly meetings on Long Island. This was my foray into Christianity.

It lasted until I found that I kept hearing things like "Let Go and Let G-d," but nobody explained what the method was for letting go. I started asking questions. The response was basically "G-d is unknowable." I knew that was not true as I had seen the face of G-d and knew that he was accessible.

My search took me through New Age literature and books. This is about the time I started teaching New Age classes for Adult Ed. I caught some slack from my fellow teachers for telling my students that they didn't need psychics and crystals or secret mantras or anything external. All they needed to do was look within.

I was already a Buddhist but I didn't know it.

I tried many different paths including a fundamentalist Christian Bible Study group in Tennessee, and Grad school in California with a major in Consciousness Studies at J.F.K University. I went through *A Course In Miracles* but found similar issues as I had found with the Cayce group.

Truth, which I had lived with intimately, is something totally alive and present. It never compromises and is always 100% true in all cases. It does not bend itself for the convenience of our egos, but shines as an example of what we are. We are not compromised shallow beings whose only concerns are our own comfort and advancement. Truth is something that defies static definitions, since it is a living and growing thing. The second you define it you lose it. I came to a point where

I believed I would never find an organized religion in which I could find a path to ultimate Truth.

Then I found Buddhism. I had known of Buddhism but rejected it when I was told, mistakenly, that at the heart of Buddhism is the idea that all of life is suffering. I was also, frankly, turned off by the insistence of Buddhists to fetishly overuse Sanskrit and Pali words. It was too reminiscent of spending hours in shul hearing and saying stuff in Hebrew that I did not understand. It made no sense to me.

Then I discovered the Tao. A wonderful and ancient book with hundreds of verses that spoke in beautiful little paradoxes like, "The Name which can be named is not the eternal Name." I thought, "Hey, that sounds a lot like Truth." As I started investigating the Tao I came upon the words of the Buddha. It was love at first sight.

I have been a practicing Buddhist for over twenty years now, and have made it my goal to bring out the Truth. I want to make this wonderful system accessible to everyone. I have applied it in my work as an actor by creating a podcast called *Zenprov*, which my wife and I have been producing for six years now. I also created a Political Zen radio talk show called *Awakened America*, which ran for two years in Chicago.

My wife and I were hired to perform Improv Comedy on a cruise going through Asia. I decided it might be a good thing to offer a course on Buddhism for Americans and Europeans that was accessible and understandable to the average Western lay-person, who has had limited exposure to the ideas contained within Buddhism. The result was Buddhism 101, which was surprisingly and overwhelmingly received with enthusiastic approval. In fact, it is because of the many requests I got in teaching that course that I wrote this book.

It is my intention to give reader the most important basic essentials of Buddhist thought. This is not an exhaustive treatise on the intricacies and ramifications of obscure Eastern thought, but an attempt to present what I have found to be a supremely practical and beautiful set of ideas to the majority of the Western people who I believe need to hear this the most.

PART 1

Meet the Buddha

CHAPTER ONE

The Life Of The Buddha

True Nature

Once there was a young woman who loved a songbird. Everyday the bird would sing outside of her window and his song was so beautiful and soulful that it made her heart joyous just to hear it.

One day her father told her that they were going to have to move to another house, but the thought of leaving the beautiful songbird behind was unbearable to her. So she began putting breadcrumbs on her windowsill, waiting for the bird to come and partake. When he did, she slowly started leaving a trail of breadcrumbs that led to a large beautiful golden birdcage. Once the bird had entered the cage she closed the door and her heart leapt for joy. She told the bird that she had to move and couldn't bear to be without him, so she was going to take him with her and that she would take very good care of him.

When they moved to the new house she set the birdcage on the windowsill so that he could look out and feel like he was free. She asked him to sing for her, for he had not done so since she caged him. *He began to sing but his song was so sad and so plaintive that it broke her heart to hear it. She knew then that it was unfair of her to expect the bird to forget his nature and be contented with captivity.*

She so loved the bird that she opened the window and then opened the cage and told him to fly away. She missed him terribly that first night and cried because she thought she would never hear his song again. But with the morning sun she began to hear his familiar beautiful song. Her bird friend had made a home in the tree outside her window and he sang of his rapture to be back where he belonged. The young woman knew she had done the right thing and shared in his joy.

What is a Buddha?

Before I tell you about the life of the Buddha, I should probably address the question, "What exactly is a Buddha?"

It is common and understandable when dealing with religions to mistake a title for a name or an identity. For example, do you know that Jesus Christ was not the founder of Christianity's name? He was a guy named Yeshua Ben Yosef, who in the course of his life became a great spiritual leader. Because of this, he was called "the anointed one," which in Greek is "Christi." Therefore "Yeshua" (or "Jesus" if you Romanize it) became the Christ, or Jesus Christ for short.

In much the same way, the Buddha is a title and not a name.

Siddhartha Gautama became the Buddha, which means "Awakened One." According to him, he was not the first or the last Buddha to appear in the world - only the most recent. Some Buddhist traditions identify 10,000 Buddhas. This number of course should be taken with a few grains of sodium. The Tao Te Ching also uses the number 10,000 as it refers to all the manifestations in the world. Of course if we think about it, Lao Tsu, the author of the Tao, knew there were more than ten thousand things in the world but he used the number much as we today may say a gazillion things. It was basically picking a number that was beyond the conception of ordinary people of that time. So as with the Buddha, 10,000 is not an actual count but signifies many more than you could count. It is also said, that each new Buddha arises once every 5,000 years, which would imply Buddhas manifesting for 5 million years. Like most dogma in religious tradition, it doesn't make logical sense, since archeological records only have Homo Sapiens for thousands, not millions, of years. But what can I say? I'm just reporting what I have heard.

Siddhartha's Conception

Siddhartha Gautama's life story begins in Nepal in a Kingdom called Kosala. The King and head of the Shakya clan was a man named Suddhodana, and his queen was Mahamaya. The Shakyas were part of the warrior caste in India. One night, Mahamaya dreamed that she was carried by four spirits to a sacred lake in the Himalayas and there bathed by them. A White Elephant then appeared, circled her several times, and entered her womb on the right side. This white elephant symbolized the Buddha himself. Thus the spirit of the Buddha manifested as a child that would be born to the King and Queen in her dream. To be clear, this was not a virgin birth. The dream merely told the Queen that she was pregnant with a very special child.

Mahamaya Dreams of the Buddha

Siddhartha's Birth

As was custom in those days, the Queen set off for her parents' home to bear the new Prince. On the way, her party stopped at the Lumbini Garden, and there under a Sal tree Siddhartha was born in 563 B.C.E. Seven days later, Queen Mahamaya died, and her sister Prajapatti became the person who raised Siddhartha. Part of Buddhist tradition says that this death of the mother after seven days is a sign of a Buddha's birth.

Signs and Portents

King Suddhodana was very excited to finally have an heir (he and the Queen had produced no children in 20 years of marriage) and called in soothsayers to predict the path his son's life would take. They all agreed the prince would be the greatest king the world had ever seen. They saw him uniting all the kingdoms under his rule. India in those days was not one contiguous country but a collection of smaller kingdoms and republics.

Then an old hermit named Asita, a very holy man, came to the palace, viewed the child and wept. When the King asked him what was wrong, he told the King that he had waited his whole life to see the Buddha. Now he had seen him but was sad that he would not live long enough to hear the Buddha teach. The King told him he must be mistaken and told him what all the other soothsayers had said.

Asita replied that the prince had two possible paths, as a great King who would unite all of India or a great spiritual master who would save the world.

Asita Foretells the Buddha's Destiny

The King's Plan

Put yourself in the King's place for a moment. He hears that he has an heir who will either take his family's kingdom and create of it a center of worldly power beyond his wildest dreams, or become a super monk. Which one would you prefer? Remember his entire life and upbringing in the warrior caste trained him to look at earthly power and domination as the goal of his entire family back to his distant ancestors.

Let's put this in terms we modern folk can relate to. Suppose you own a hardware store that was created by your great grandfather and has been handed down through the generations. You want to keep it going within the family. Thankfully you now have a son to whom you can pass the family business on to. Everyone who comes into the store and meets your son talks about what a natural hardware man he will be. They predict great things for him and the store. They see him as growing the business into a multinational franchise. Then one day a homeless man enters your store and says to you, "Yes it is possible he will be this great hardware man but he might also become the head of the Hari Krishnas at the airport."

The King's reaction was quite understandable. He wanted to make sure his son chose the "right" path, so he determined to make sure that Siddhartha never experienced any suffering nor was exposed to anyone else suffering around him. In this way, he believed he could stifle Siddhartha's natural inclinations towards compassion and the spiritual, and keep his feet firmly planted in the life of a warrior king. From the earliest age, the boy was shielded from any unpleasantness and given everything the King could think of to keep him satisfied in order to tie him to the royal life.

Despite the King's best efforts, young Siddhartha had a life-altering experience when placed under a tree during a festival. While sitting there, he entered what could rightly be described as a meditative state and became aware of his connection to all beings and all things. This experience would come back to him later in life.

He grew from a baby into a man, and was married to Yasodhara before ever seeing that there was anything else but his royal lifestyle. The King continued to shelter Siddhartha from anything other than pleasures and ease. No old or sick people were ever allowed in his son's presence, and certainly no monks or holy men. Siddhartha was shielded from the experience of anyone dying as well. He was kept totally ignorant of any of these things for most of his young life.

The Four Messengers

One day Siddhartha told his father that he wanted to go out with his charioteer for a look at the surrounding countryside, village and the people. The King loved his son and did not want to keep him as a prisoner so he agreed. The King tried to control what Siddhartha would see by planning the entire route and putting forth a major effort to ensure Siddhartha would only encounter good and pleasant sights. But the King, try as he might, could not account for every contingency.

As Siddhartha and Chana (his charioteer) made their way, Siddhartha saw a fragile old man slowly making his way along the road. Siddhartha stopped the charioteer and asked him what it was he was seeing, for he had never encountered an old person before. "That is an old person, my Prince," came the reply. "We all grow old. Even you will grow old one day." Siddhartha was shocked, as you may imagine.

Siddhartha sees the Aging, Illness, Death and a Monk

They continued their ride and eventually came upon a weakened person lying by the side of the road. "What is that?" Siddhartha exclaimed, having never seen a sick person before. "That is a sick person," the charioteer explained. "All people experience sickness. Even you will experience sickness, my Prince."

Shaken, Siddhartha continued the ride until they came across a funeral procession bearing a dead body. Once again Siddhartha questioned the charioteer. "Chana, what the heck is that?" "That is a dead person. Sooner or later we all die. Even you, my Prince," was the reply.

On they went and Siddhartha's eyes came upon a holy man, a seeker who had renounced all possessions in search of ultimate Truth. He told Chana to stop and got out to talk with the Holy Man. After talking to him, Siddhartha determined that he would become a holy man and seek to find the way out of the suffering that he now understood all living beings experienced due to these three things he had seen; sickness, old age and death.

The New Path

Siddhartha, although he really wanted to, did not immediately set out to become a seeker of Truth, but the seed that had been planted during that chariot ride found fertile ground and was growing larger and more insistent everyday. Being a person of great compassion, it was hard for him to shatter his father's plans, leave his young wife whom he loved most dearly and the new son she had borne him. He had named the boy Rahula, which can be translated as "impediment" or "fetter," because he felt the birth of his son would keep him from following what he knew he must do. One night he crept into Yasodhara's room to take a last look at her and the child. He knew that if he woke them, he would never go. He quietly left the palace and struck out on a new path, as a renunciate and seeker of Truth. He determined that he would return when he found the Way and free those he loved.

A Last Look at his Wife and Child

Renunciation

Siddhartha set his feet upon a new path. He left his horse to be returned to the palace by his trusted servant, Chana, who accompanied him on his midnight escape. He took off his heavy gold earrings which had stretched his earlobes, and traded them and his expensive clothing for a monk's robe and a begging bowl. He used his sword to cut his long hair and set out on the path of a seeker of Truth.

Teachers

Siddhartha sought out the two best and wisest teachers in the land. He studied with these teachers and within a relatively short time mastered their lessons. These were disciplines of the mind that usually took years to master, if they were mastered at all, but Siddhartha did so relatively quickly and easily. In each case, his newly achieved profound state of mind still left him with unanswered questions about how to overcome suffering.

The teachers were so impressed by him that they offered to have him as a co-teacher, a great honor to be sure. But Siddhartha found that each time he mastered a new technique, the suffering was still with him. He was not yet free. He had not found the way.

After these disappointments with the teachers, he determined to try something else. He came to understand that if these, the greatest Teachers available could not help him find the Way, it left him no choice but to find the answers himself. He left with five other fellow students to try the path of self-denial.

Asceticism

In India at that time and still today, it is believed that suffering comes from having a body. If you could free yourself from the incessant demands and desires and constant tending of the body, you could find liberation. It was thought that by denying and mortifying the flesh, one could overcome all physical needs and desires and become free of them.

So Siddhartha decided to walk the path of extreme asceticism. He, along with his group of five other seekers, practiced radical austerities such as denying themselves food and comfort of all types. Siddhartha would go into the woods alone at night and sit shivering from fear and exposure. He lived for a while on one grain of rice a day. As a result, Siddhartha dwindled from the healthy and beautiful princely young man he had been to a skeleton with skin stretched tightly across it. At one point he became so weak that he fell down by a river and was near death.

Siddhartha Practices Asceticism

As he lay there dying, it came to him that even practicing the most extreme form of self denial had not freed him from suffering. A young girl who was bringing milk for an offering to the gods came across him and fed him. She nursed him back to health and Siddhartha decided to end his life of asceticism.

The Middle Way

Siddhartha had lived a life of luxury and ease having everything he could ever desire, had learned from all the great teachers and all forms of intellectual and spiritual practice available to him, practiced the most extreme forms of self denial, and yet still failed to find the end of suffering. This left him wondering how he was to achieve liberation. Siddhartha remembered from playing the lute that a string stretched too tight would break and a string too loose would produce no music. His former life as a Prince was the string strung too loosely and his life as an ascetic was the string tuned too tightly. He realized that the correct path was a path not of extremes, which, like the lute string, made the instrument of his body and mind dysfunctional, but of moderation.

He remembered his early experience of sitting under the tree at the festival and how he entered a serene and profound state where he felt at one with everything.

With this realization, he determined to sit beneath a nearby beautiful fig tree and vowed not to stop until he achieved enlightenment. During this time, his five former ascetic brothers saw him and left, thinking he had abandoned the spiritual path.

Becoming the Buddha

There is some disagreement as to how long Siddhartha sat under the Bodhi tree (tree of awakening) to attain enlightenment, but it was somewhere between one night and forty days. Whatever the time, the story is as follows:

One night, Siddhartha achieved a deep state of relaxation and meditation. While in that state, Mara, the Hindu god of illusion that symbolizes the ego and the small self within each of us, tried to distract and disrupt Siddhartha's meditation. He tried everything from sending his three voluptuous daughters to seduce Siddhartha, to having his demon hordes attack and try to distract him. But Siddhartha remained unmoved and still.

Finally, Mara declared that he, Mara, deserved to be honored as the enlightened one and had all of his demons cheering and supporting him. Mara challenged Siddhartha. "I have all these hordes who support my claim. Who supports you?" Siddhartha simply reached down and touched the earth with his fingers asking it to bear witness to the Truth. The earth trembled in response, and Mara was defeated. (Many statues of the Buddha depict this moment showing him sitting in meditation with his right hand reaching down to touch the earth.)

With the rising of the morning star, Siddhartha realized the full Truth and achieved perfect enlightenment, becoming the Buddha in 528 B.C.E. As a part of his enlightenment experience, the veil of forgetfulness was lifted from his mind and he saw all of his past lives in all different forms leading up to this moment. He understood clearly the true nature of reality and was free from suffering for the first time in his life. He had achieved liberation. From this time forward he is no longer called Siddhartha but is called the Buddha for now he is the Awakened One.

Siddhartha Becomes the Buddha

What To Do with Enlightenment?

So now Siddhartha was the Buddha. He was free of suffering and saw the path that would free anyone from suffering. What he did not know, however, was whether or not anyone would understand what it was he had to teach.

His first attempt to teach a seeker he met on the road was less than impressive, and the Buddha had serious doubts as to whether he would be able to transmit his knowledge.

This occurred shortly after his enlightenment when he happened upon another monk walking down the road. As was custom when two monks meet, this monk asked the Buddha who his teacher was and what had he learned. The Buddha replied that he had no teacher and that he had found the way to perfect liberation. The other monk reacted the way someone would when they come across someone who sounds like a nut. With a, "Well isn't that nice for you, oh look at the time I have to be going" or something to that effect, the monk walked away from the Buddha.

The Buddha realized at this point that not everyone was ready to hear the Truth. He thought about it and realized that he would teach those who had only a little dust covering their eyes so he could help clear their vision and help them see. Still, he wasn't sure he could do it.

With his great compassion, however, he resolved to try. He sought out the five ascetic brothers who had left him before and resolved to teach them. At first they were hostile, but upon hearing the Buddha's words they all achieved enlightenment and became his first successful students.

He taught them the Four Noble Truths, which is what forms the heart of Buddhism and which we will cover later in greater depth, but in short what he told them was: Suffering exists, Suffering has a cause, Suffering can be ended, and, finally, how to end it.

Teaching the Dharma till He Was 80

For the next 45 years the Buddha lived as a monk, teaching and setting up and administering monasteries developed from his growing ranks of followers across the region. These followers were called Bikkhus, which translates literally as "beggar." Those who were accepted as monks gave up all worldly possessions and positions, spent time in meditation and service, and begged for their food once a day from local villagers and in return would offer teaching and blessings.

Eventually he returned to the palace, as he had promised, to share what he found with his family. Most of the Buddha's family, including his aunt, wife and son, became monks and nuns (Bikkhunis). In fact, it was Prajapatti, his aunt and the woman who raised him, who argued and lobbied for the Buddha to accept women into his monasteries, something he was hesitant to do as it was such a radical break from custom at the time. She asked him if he thought it was not possible for a woman to achieve liberation and he affirmed that this was not the case. She became his first nun.

The Buddha confronted a notorious serial killer, Angulimala, by walking right up to him when others were terrified to do so, and converted him on the spot. Angulimala means necklace of fingers. He earned this name because he would cut of a finger of each person he killed. When the Buddha spoke to him, Angulimala became Ahimsaka and one of his most devout and peaceful monks. ("Ahimsa" is the way of non-violence.)

Buddha Converts the Serial Killer Angulimala

The Buddha advised kings and princes, went against custom to accept untouchables and reject the caste system, and survived scandals based on lies by remaining constant and saying that the Truth would win out eventually, which it did.

Ascendancy to Paranirvana at 80

At the age of 80, the Buddha passed from this life. It was his custom, though he was a vegetarian and fairly strict about his diet, to eat whatever had been prepared for him so as not to embarrass a host who had sought to honor him. This included his last meal of poisonous mushrooms, which he knew were bad but ate anyway. It is not clear whether he did this to keep from embarrassing the host or because he felt it was time for him to go.

In either case, when you see a statue depicting the Buddha lying on his side or reclining, this is a depiction of his dying scene in which he is surrounded by monks and giving a final lesson. The monks wailed and asked what they were to do without their teacher. He reminded them that the Dharma was with them, and as long as they held to the Dharma they would be all right. He reminded them that he was just a messenger and not to be worshipped. "Do not mistake the finger pointing at the Moon for the Moon itself." He was the pointing finger; the Dharma was the Moon itself.

The Buddha Bids Farewell to his Followers

He reiterated what had been the theme of his entire course of teaching through the years - that all things are impermanent. "Work diligently on your liberation," were his final words. He then died and ascended to Paranirvana. His final lesson was that nothing was to be clung to, even him.

How Do We Have His Words and Life Story?

The Buddha did not write down any of his teachings, nor anything else for that matter. He was very concerned that his teaching would be turned into a religion and that the core of what he had been teaching would transform from live words of incredible wisdom to dead utterances of dogma.

When he said, "Do not mistake the finger pointing at the moon for the moon itself," he meant that he was the one pointing at the moon but he wanted us to know that it was the moon that mattered, not the pointer.

On another occasion he said, "To cross a river one must build a raft, but once you reach the other side, one does not carry the raft on one's back." Again, he was talking about the importance of what he was teaching and stressing the fact that what he was doing was creating a guide to get us to a place of liberation, while reminding us that the function of the map or the teaching or even the person of the Buddha himself was to be discarded once we reached our goal.

So how do we manage to know so much about the teachings and life of this man that lived 2,600 years ago?

It so happened that the Buddha had a personal assistant named Ananda who devoted his life to serving the Buddha. Ananda was the Buddha's cousin and a member of the Shakya clan. Many of Buddha's noble relatives became Bhikkus after he returned to Kapilivatu, his former home. Once the Buddha passed, a group of senior monks got together and decided it would be a good idea to chronicle the life and teachings of the Buddha for posterity. As it turned out, Ananda was possessed with the facility of eidetic imagery, or photographic memory. This was the reason why he was assigned to be the Buddha's servant - so that he could record in his memory everything the Buddha said.

It is from Ananda that we have most of the Buddha's history and teachings, as well as from others involved in that project.

Other Buddhas?

The Buddha we speak of when discussing the Buddha is actually Gautama Buddha or Shakyamuni Buddha, but he is neither the first or last Buddha. Buddha is a title, not a name, which means "Awakened One" and is something we can all aspire to become. The most recent to become the Buddha was Siddhartha Gautama 2,600 years ago. It is said a Buddha appears every 5,000 years or so, when the Dharma (the Truth that the Buddha teaches) disappears from the consciousness of mankind.

The next Buddha is said to be Maietreya who is sometimes depicted as one of his past lives as the fat jolly monk many people often mistakenly think of as the current Buddha. Repeat, the fat jolly man that people mistakenly call the laughing Buddha is not a Buddha at all. He was a monk who was known as the sack cloth monk because he always carried a sack made of cloth from which he would distribute gifts to the children.

Not the Buddha

The Sackcloth Monk - Buddhai

CHAPTER TWO

What the Buddha Taught

How To See Everything

There was once a curious young man who went to the village sage and asked him how he could see everything. The sage thought for a moment and then told the young man that if he were to climb to the top of a mountain he would see everything. Now the village was situated in the flat plains of the lowland, so the young one did not know what a mountain was. He asked the sage and the sage told him, "It is a part of the earth that rises to a very great height and from the top you can see everything."

Excited to begin his quest, the young man set out right away and travelled for many miles before he came to a small hillock. "This must be a mountain," he thought. "I will climb it and see everything. So climb it he did, but when he got to the top he was disappointed to find that though he could see more than he could on the plains, he still could not see everything.

He continued his quest and before too long he came to a low hill. "Aha, this must be a mountain", he mused, "I will climb it and see everything from there." But just as before, though he could see more than he could see on the hillock, it was most certainly not everything.

Again he came upon a hill that was much higher than the one before. He cautiously climbed the great hill suspecting that this would prove no better than the others had, and it turned out he was correct. Though he could see more, he still could not see everything.

He began to despair that he would ever find a mountain and see everything. Still he continued on, though his step was not as springy and his heart was not as enthusiastic as before. Just when he thought about giving up and turning around, he crested a ridge and there before him was the biggest tallest piece of earth he had ever seen. It was so large he had trouble imagining reaching the top, but he had come this far and so he determined that he would try or die.

Many, many, excruciating hours later he finally reached the top of the mountain. As he sat there, his muscles and body exhausted, he was overcome with a peace and a sense of great accomplishment. "Ah," he said. "Now I see everything."

When the Buddha began to teach after his enlightenment, his first true lesson was addressed to his five former brothers in asceticism. The content of this lesson was called the Four Noble Truths and forms the basis of what the Buddha taught.

It's All About the Suffering

The Buddha was very consistent when it came to what it was he felt was most important for him to teach, and he focused like a laser on it for the 45 years he taught. He once held up a leaf and asked the monks, "Monks, which is greater, the leaf I hold in my hand or all the leaves in this forest?" Of course the monks answered that the leaves in the forest would be the greater number. "Just so," he said. "What I teach you is like this one leaf compared to all the knowledge in the universe."

His motivation for leaving his comfortable home, wife and small child and becoming a monk was done for one reason which was consistently followed throughout his years of struggle and final enlightenment. Searching for liberation from suffering was at the heart of what he sought and found, and what he offered to those who came to learn from him. The Pali word "dukka" has usually been translated as "suffering," but it can also imply unsatisfactoriness or discomfort.

The issue comes down to birth and death. Since the knowledge of birth and death is what causes so many to suffer, he looked deeply into each. What he found comprises the Four Noble Truths which form the very foundation and structure of Buddhism.

But birth and death, he came to see, apply to absolutely everything created. Everything in the universe arises and ceases. Without exception, everything that is will one day no longer be. This was the thought that drove him to seek liberation from the endless cycle of birth and death that in turn caused so much suffering. He was certainly talking about the birth and death of all sentient beings, but even more what he was referring to was the constant frustration of being alive - wanting something and either having it denied to you outright or slipping away once you attained it. This flavors and colors all lives and leads to a state of constant loss and grieving, differing only in degree. These were the questions that confronted Siddhartha when he took that chariot ride and saw sickness, old age and death, which all beings are subject to. The answer came during his enlightenment and this is what he shared.

The First Noble Truth:
Suffering Exists

The Buddha stated that suffering exists for all sentient beings. This recognition is important because were it not so, there would be no reason to seek a way out or another way of being. If everything were hunky dory why would anyone want to evolve? Seeking liberation if there is nothing to be liberated from would be the basis of a very silly religion.

The Second Noble Truth:
There is a Cause of Suffering

Were suffering just an organic part of life and the nature of the beast, there again would be no reason to go any further. You might as well then seek to wean yourself from the need for nourishment. This is what the Buddha tried to do unsuccessfully with the path of asceticism.

But by denying himself food he did not free himself from the need for it. It was organic and not the cause of suffering. A person must eat and sleep and have shelter. If not, the body will cease to be.

Suffering on the other hand is not inextricably linked to living. It is not organic. It is something that is foreign to our true nature that we create for ourselves due to ignorance of the way things really are.

The Buddha taught that suffering is not inevitable but is completely self created and optional. This is a major thought because it implies we are creating our own problems and are therefore not victims of fate or an apathetic universe. We can actually do something to free ourselves from this suffering. The second Noble Truth expounds upon what it is that we do that causes us to suffer.

The Third Noble Truth:
The Cessation of Suffering is Possible

This is the next logical step from the second Noble Truth. If suffering is self-created and not an organic part of life, then it is possible to change whatever it is we are doing to create it in the first place. Were this not possible, again there would be no rationale for Buddhism at all. This is good news for anyone who would prefer to live without suffering.

That having been said, however, though this appears to be a simple thing to do, I would caution that it is simple but it is not easy.

The Fourth Noble Truth:
A Practical Manual for How to End Suffering

The Fourth Noble Truth is actually the most involved of the Four and was called by the Buddha, "The Noble Eightfold Path." This is where the Buddha spelled out precisely what one needed to do in order to end the cycles of suffering in one's own life and the suffering we tend to create for others as well. It entails eight qualities we must develop in ourselves to be free of suffering.

The Buddha as a Physician

Another way to look at the Four Noble Truths is by looking at suffering as a medical condition and the Buddha as a physician who wishes to treat this condition. The first step in medicine is to identify whether or not there is a problem. This is the diagnosis. The Buddha studied the patient (sentient beings) and concluded that there is an inorganic condition known as suffering. This is the first Noble Truth.

Next, the physician looks to see whether there is a cause for the condition. This is important, as it will lead to a strategy for combating the illness.

Again, the Buddha studied the patient and determined that yes, there was a clear identifiable cause for this condition of suffering. This is the second Noble Truth.

Having taken this step, Dr. Buddha sought to determine whether this condition was treatable or not. After all, a doctor can diagnose a condition, find a cause for that condition and then determine the condition is terminal. In this case, happily, the Buddha did indeed find that there was a cure for the condition. The third Noble Truth.

At the heart of his six-year search was experimentation and searching for the cure, just as a doctor in a lab would experiment and search for effective means to cure the illness. Once these other steps have been taken, the doctor prescribes some form of treatment that he has discovered through his laboratory experiments and found to be efficacious. This manifests in Buddhism as the fourth Noble Truth, the Noble Eightfold Path.

Luckily, the Buddha was not actually a Doctor or there would have been a fifth Noble Truth where he presents you with the bill.

Breaking it Down

Here's the idea behind the Four Noble Truths. You are not going to Hell in some future existence because you were bad. At any time, you can leave and live in paradise. All it takes is changing your mind and behavior. Hell, in other words, is a self-imposed experience that is present and utterly escapable.

It is like living in New Jersey. Having grown up in New York City, no fate seems worse to me than living in New Jersey. Nobody actually wants to live in New Jersey, but because of other ties you have (family, work, etc.) it is the place you can afford and so it is where you end up. The longer you live there the harder it becomes to make a change. Before you know it, you are an actual New Jerseyite, (I have no earthly idea what a person who lives in New Jersey is actually called except perhaps unfortunate.) You are aware of the smell of the refineries and the traffic and the congestion and the dirt and the noise and... well, you get the idea. And yet you feel as though you simply can not leave because of things that appear to you to be absolutely integral to your life. So you continue to live in New Jersey and suffer all of the indignities that go with it. All of the things you cling to as "necessities," and all of the things you seek to avoid, trap you in the narrow choice of continuing to live in the Garden State.

If, though, you were to decide at some point that the job and the family and the security and the house and all the other ten thousand things that keep you there are no longer worth the price you have to pay to live there, you are then free to move to Bermuda. It's really not hard to get there. I have sailed from Cape Liberty in New Jersey to Bermuda many times. It can be done.

So using my poor example here, you can understand that suffering (in this case living in New Jersey) exists. The First Noble Truth. There is a cause for living in New Jersey, which in this case manifests as a host of reasons you are attached to a particular life that is possible only in New Jersey. That is the second Noble Truth. It is possible to move out of New Jersey. That would be the Third Noble Truth. And then you go and buy a one-way ticket to Bermuda. Now you are liberated from New Jersey.

If you are from a different part of the world and can not relate to being stuck in New Jersey, try replacing New Jersey with lets say, Texas or Mississippi or some other G-d-forsaken place you wouldn't want to be.

Suffering Exists

The first thing the Buddha taught was that suffering, as a condition, exists. This might not sound like much but it is the basis upon which all his other teachings are built. This is what sent him out searching and looking for an answer to how to cure suffering which, he said, exists. Suffering is distinct from existential sadness. It is not the same thing. Sadness is something that is an inevitable part of life as a sentient being, as opposed to suffering which is added on to the experience of life and is entirely optional.

Let me say that again. Sadness is inevitable. It is a part of life. It comes from loving and caring for that which changes and disappears. Sadness is an emotion which we experience as part of a process of grieving. If we do not try to stop the process, we feel the sadness. We have a good cleansing cry, and through it are restored to our balanced selves. Suffering is something we add on after the sadness, but is not necessary or inevitable nor does it have the cleansing quality of sadness. It is a feeling of stuckness and wrongness. Think of the word "emotion." If you take away the 'e', that leaves you with motion. This is significant because emotional states are not static things. They do not last very long but are subject to dynamic processes that when complete naturally lead to release and acceptance. Suffering is the tension and stress we feel when we try to block the emotional process and don't allow it to complete.

There is a Cause of Suffering

When I first heard about Buddhism, I was told that it was based on the idea that all of life is suffering. Not surprisingly, I had no interest in exploring it further. I mean, I grew up in Judaism where suffering is a high art. I'd had enough of suffering. But it turned out that what I had been told was wrong.

The Buddha did not think that life was unavoidably about suffering. What he said was that all sentient beings experience suffering in the course of our lives, but that we cause our own suffering and therefore we have the power to end it as well. Buddhism is actually about the end of suffering. I liked that idea a whole lot better.

The Cause of Suffering

So if suffering is not inevitable and it has a cause and we have a say in whether or not we suffer, what the heck is it that we are doing that causes us to suffer? To answer this question we have to go a little deeper into the Buddha's teaching on the nature of reality. It is because of our basic ignorance of the nature of reality that we unknowingly cause all of this suffering in the first place. We will discuss this in more depth in a later chapter.

Suffice it to say, the Buddha identified the cause of suffering as clinging and avoidance. Basically, fear. Clinging to or avoiding whatever it is that has manifested or ceased to manifest in your life leads to the formation of suffering.

Experiencing a loss, for example, of a loved one is naturally followed by a reaction of sadness and a sense of loss. Left alone, this process will play itself out through grieving, and normalcy will return when the process completes itself. If, however, we cannot accept the loss of this loved one and we refuse to grieve because we have not accepted the reality of the loss, then we have stopped the dynamic process of life. When we do this we begin to experience suffering on top of the sadness.

Likewise, if we live in fear of something happening and work to avoid it, we are clinging to that thing not happening which, inevitably, it will and in its turn cause suffering. Say you're working at a job where you do not feel secure. You spend all of your time being afraid of being fired. Nothing has happened at that point but you have begun to worry preemptively.

In both these instances the natural flow of life's processes are fought against and we experience this within the body as stress and tension. This is what suffering feels like.

Suffering Can Be Ended

So what I had been told many years ago, that Buddhism was all about how suffering was just a part of life, was wrong, a perversion of the truth. The actual basis of Buddhism is that suffering does indeed exist, and it is ubiquitous due to the inevitability of certain things happening to which we are either clinging and grasping, or avoiding and seeking to keep at bay. This is unnecessary and can be ended. Since suffering has a knowable cause and since the cause is attributable to us, it follows logically that we in turn can change what we are doing and live without suffering.

We are creatures of habit and walk through our lives barely conscious of what we are doing or thinking at any particular moment. Too many of us live our lives on autopilot, reacting reflexively to any stimulus and thereby wearing huge ruts in the paths of our lives that can seem impossible to crawl out of. Eventually we create a rut so deep that we cannot even see above the surface.

We have no idea that we are living on a very narrow track and so we keep doing the same things as though we had no other choice. There appear to be levels upon levels of consciousness, much of which is so deeply repressed we feel we can never reach it all. These levels are nothing more than the silent awareness that life is so much bigger and better than we are living it. When we sleepwalk through our day we miss the beautiful variety and complexity of life.

And yet in order to effect change we *must* become conscious of what motivates our actions, or we are doomed to keep repeating mistakes which only lead to more suffering. This cycle of mindless habitual behaviors is the way most of us operate. It is why we find ourselves suffering from the same mistakes over and over again.

This is why the Buddha set out to find the way so many years ago and this is, indeed, what he eventually found. No matter how hard and even impossible it may seem, there is a way out of the cycle of suffering. This disease can be cured. The sleepwalking can be overcome. It is why he is called the Awakened One. Every step he took, was taken in complete awareness.

The Way Out

The Buddha laid out a succinct and specific plan for how one may end suffering in their lives and the lives of others: The Noble Eightfold Path. If the first three Noble Truths can be seen as the definition of the problem, the fourth is the solution to the problem.

It is easy to say we are creating our own suffering with the obvious conclusion that we should stop doing that, but as I said, this is one of those examples where the answer is easy to say but perhaps not as easy to do. In order to stop creating suffering in our lives, we must change habits that have become so deeply ingrained and resistant to change that we are not even aware that we have other choices. If you can't see the alternatives and aren't consciously aware of the alternatives, how can you choose an alternative?

If the cause of the problem is in our day-to-day thinking and actions, then the first thing we have to do is become aware of what it is we are doing. We must become consciously aware of how we think and how we behave. It means we have to stop and microscopically examine our whole psyche and modus operandi. It means retraining our mind and body to perform in an effective manner by first becoming aware of how we are not doing that. It means overcoming all emotional attachments to continuing in the same rut that has by now become familiar and safe and, despite any rational proof to the contrary, we need to understand that this way we have been thinking and behaving is really bad for us.

Thus the Buddha gives us the Noble Eightfold Path to show us an easier and more structured method for going about the difficult task of self-examination and change that will ultimately result in our freedom from suffering.

Right

Before we delve into the Noble Eightfold Path, I want to say a word about a word that is ubiquitous in the Noble Eightfold Path. It's a word fraught with contextual misunderstandings and could lead you astray from the outset.

Let us go back to New Jersey (don't worry this is a short visit). Say you wanted to get the heck out of New Jersey and rather than a GPS you have a person in the passenger seat directing you while reading a map. When they say turn left because it is the right way to go, there is no moral judgment in that. This is just a simple statement of fact.

In the same way the use of the word "Right," which appears in every step of the path, should not be read as "right vs. wrong" in a moral sense. There is no judgment here about one's character or prudishness, with a wagging finger telling us we are bad and will be punished if we don't do what we're told.

In the Noble Eightfold Path, the word "right" should be understood as meaning "correct" as opposed to "incorrect" in a very neutral fashion. There is an assumption on the part of the Buddha that you want to find your way out of suffering and he is supplying a road map for you. The Buddha is the person sitting in the passenger seat telling you which roads and turns will lead you out of New Jersey, and which will just get you more lost in the usual confusing New Jersey way.

Anyone who has ever driven through Newark and mistakenly gotten off an exit only to find they can never find their way back to where they were will understand what I am saying here. I personally think this is how New Jersey gets people to move there in the first place. They just get so lost and hopeless trying to find their way out that they eventually give up and find a house.

But I digress.

You understand when the Buddha navigating from the passenger seat says, "this is the right way," he is not making a statement regarding your moral fiber, but simply telling you that the road you're on will lead where you want to go. No more than that should be read into the word "right" when looking at the Noble Eightfold Path. It is "right" as in correct for the specific purpose of liberating yourself from suffering. (Or, if you like the metaphor, getting out of New Jersey.)

The Noble Eightfold Path

1. Right View
2. Right Intention
3. Right Speech
4. Right Action
5. Right Livelihood
6. Right Effort
7. Right Mindfulness
8. Right Concentration

Suffice it to say you should not be surprised that the Noble Eightfold Path is composed of eight items. See? This stuff is easy.

These eight items are further classified into three categories: Wisdom (view and intention), Ethical Conduct (speech, action and livelihood), and finally Mental Development (effort, mindfulness and concentration).

WISDOM

Right View

Right View refers to the essential understanding that one must have in order to free oneself from suffering.

You first need to understand that you create your own suffering and the mechanisms which make this so. Understandings of impermanence, interdependency and emptiness of self (which will be explained in depth in a later chapter) must be applied to all things so that you can see your way clear to freedom. Ignorance is the one thing that keeps us in bondage to suffering, therefore it is important to address ignorance as to the nature of reality in order to find your way to clarity.

Right Intention

In this step, the Buddha is referring to the level of one's commitment to making the changes necessary to effect liberation. It is fine to understand that a certain behavior is counter-productive and even harmful, but without the strong intention of doing something to change that behavior, nothing can be accomplished. With intention to change, nothing can stand in your way. This step refers specifically to the idea of walking in a rut.

We are creatures of habit. When you get an itch you do not think, "Gee I have this sensation on my nose which I find disturbing. Hmm, what can I do about this? Aha I have these nails on the end of my fingers that can be used to address this sensation." At least I hope you don't. No, what happens is that the itch and the scratch happen almost simultaneously. It's really case of Itch-Scratch. One of the first things you learn when meditating in a Zen Monastery is that once you begin a meditation session you may not move. I can tell you from personal experience how powerful and deeply ingrained the urge to scratch an itch is. This is an example of a habitual behavior or action. There really is no thought expended here, just a reflexive response to a certain stimulus. Now apply this to all of the things you do in a non-conscious habitual way and you begin to understand why Right Intention is so important.

ETHICAL CONDUCT

Right Speech

Words that we utter to others have actual force and power, and lead to either a reduction or an increase in the suffering of others, and of ourselves.

We have all had the experience of saying something to someone and realizing after we said it that we have either hurt them or hurt another. This can happen often when we are angry. "I just said it without thinking." How many times have you heard or said that?

Before we speak, we need to think about what we are about to say. Is it true? If not don't say it. Is it meant to be helpful? If not, don't say it. Is it likely to be helpful despite the intention? If not, don't say it. Is it likely to lead to a release from further suffering for the other or yourself? Is it timely? If not, don't say it. The point here is to become mindful of the power of our speech and to work to ensure that the only speech we perform is that which is most likely to lead to the end of suffering for ourselves and others. It is better to remain silent and cause no harm than to speak without thinking and cause more suffering.

Right Action

As with speech, our actions can have powerful repercussions on those around us and ourselves. We need to train ourselves not to act until we are certain that what we are about to do will most likely lead to an end of suffering for ourselves and others.

This does not mean that we should always do what is popular or pleasing. In the context of dealing with an addict, certainly the most pleasing thing you could do in the short term would be to make drugs as available as possible, but in the long run this will only prolong their suffering. Sometimes it is kinder to be hard. We must do our best to be truly helpful in what we do.

It is also better to wait and be sure than to act precipitously and cause harm.

Right Livelihood

Earning money by the sweat of our brow is an essential human activity and one that is fairly universal. Too often, though, we are asked to compromise ideals in the service of making a living. As with speech and action, we must examine whether what we do for our livelihood adds to or subtracts from the suffering in others and in us.

In this area, the Buddha got fairly specific and mentioned a few types of livelihood by name that were not considered Right Livelihood:

1. Dealing in weapons, because this most definitely leads to the harm of other sentient beings. You

don't have to commit the act in order to suffer from it. If you make it possible for someone else to do harm, it is as though you have done it yourself.

2. Dealing in living beings (including raising animals for slaughter as well as slave trade and prostitution.) Remember, not causing suffering applies to all sentient beings - not just humans.

3. Working in meat production and butchery.

4. Selling intoxicants and poisons, such as alcohol and drugs. The Buddha asked all of his followers to take certain precepts in order to be accepted. One of these was a prohibition on the use of intoxicants. Why? Again, the answer is very practical. You are trying to develop your mind and concentration. Using intoxicants confuses the mind and makes concentration more difficult.

Additionally, any occupation that involved conflict with the principles of right speech and right action are, not surprisingly, considered unhelpful professions to attaining freedom from suffering. This could apply to politicians who knowingly spread fear and lies in order to gain power. Many people, not knowing any better, believe these falsehoods and it harms them and others. Climate change is a perfect example of this. Climate change deniers have made it very difficult to address the very real consequences of this global challenge. As a result Suffering is increased.

MENTAL DEVELOPMENT

Right Effort

It may seem surprising that effort would be categorized as being Mental Development rather than a form of conduct, but in this case we are discussing effort in a different context than merely doing. It is said that desire is the engine for everything. Certainly without desire nothing would ever be accomplished.

Contrary to popular belief, Buddhism is not about the extinguishing of all desires but about the harnessing of this powerful energy source in the service of freeing oneself. Just as a rocket must have a narrowly focused tube to direct the incredible energy of its engine, desire must be narrowly focused in order to move in a consistent direction. If one's desires are all over the place, the person will likewise find their life unfocused and drifting in many directions, getting them nowhere.

Right Effort is about the focusing of your desire on the sole purpose of freeing yourself from suffering. There is a form of gravity that keeps us orbiting the same habitual way of living and keeps us within the sphere of suffering. In order to leave this orbit and move toward Nirvana, one must have a focused and functioning engine to achieve escape velocity.

Thich Nhat Hanh, a Vietnamese Buddhist Master uses the example of seeds to illustrate how mental effort works and why it is so important. What he says is that within each of our minds there are the seeds for all things both good and bad. What you express and think and live is dependent upon which seeds you nurture and which you allow to wither.

The Buddha defined four general areas to focus one's effort:

1. To prevent the arising of un-arisen unwholesome states. In other words, recognizing what thoughts are undesirable and not lending any support by way of cultivation.
2. To abandon unwholesome states that have already arisen. This would be more like finding weeds in your garden and again doing nothing to support their growth.
3. To arouse wholesome states that have not yet arisen, like nurturing characteristics you find to be helpful.
4. To maintain and perfect wholesome states already arisen, like caring for your beautiful and thriving garden with love.

Right Mindfulness

Continuing the rocket metaphor, if Right Effort can be seen as the engine that moves us towards our goal of freedom, Right Mindfulness would be the navigation system that clearly sees the route we must take to get there.

One of the reasons we remain enslaved to suffering is we are not consciously aware of what is happening or what exists in the present moment. We do not clearly see how our actions and ways of thinking keep leading us down unprofitable paths, which lead to more suffering. We divorce the cause and effect and find ourselves scratching our heads when we find ourselves lost thinking, how the heck did I get here?

Right mindfulness is about being 100% aware of everything as it is in the present moment. To achieve this we must become scientific observers of ourselves. The Buddha breaks it down this way, into the *four foundations of mindfulness:*

1. Contemplation of the body
2. Contemplation of feeling (pleasant, unpleasant, or neutral)
3. Contemplation of the state of mind, and
4. Contemplation of the phenomena (everything that manifests.)

When we understand the language of the body and its feelings, when we understand the deepest inner workings of our minds and the true nature of reality, only then can we successfully navigate our way free of suffering.

Right Concentration

This is perhaps the most ethereal of all of the steps of the Noble Eightfold Path, as it refers to a mental faculty that has been woefully underdeveloped and misunderstood in our Western culture.

According to the Buddha, the mind is the birthplace of all things. Everything arises out of the mind. As we are not usually trained to focus and calm our minds, what arises in most of our lives is chaotic and seemingly without rhyme or reason. This perfectly reflects the scattered nature of our unfocused mental state.

The practice of meditation, which is just beginning to gain limited acceptance in the West, is the practice of developing control and precision over this extremely powerful source of creation. As we sit in meditation everyday, we begin to quiet the quasi-insane and uncontrolled ramblings that run through our minds like a radio tuned between stations, picking up cross-chatter and noise, most of which is unintelligible and useless.

It is like having seven radios lined up and turned on. The loudest one is all you can hear because it drowns out the others. As we quiet each radio we become able to hear the quieter more subtle radios and what they are saying. As we sit in meditation, we retune the radio to the one station that broadcasts the quietest and wisest programming, which is always available to all of us. More on this later.

This Dharma that is the same as the quietest radio is the only thing that can truly instruct you. There are teachers and sources of information and programs and therapists and friends and lovers, and rivals and enemies who all play the part of teachers, and get you part of the way there. But in the end, your inner voice is the only true guide that can take you all the way. This is the meaning of the phrase, "If you meet the Buddha on the road kill him." Even this most trusted teacher is simply pointing out the way for you but you must walk it on your own to actually reach it. We do this by training our minds through meditation.

That is the Noble Eightfold Path.

What Comes After?

What happens after you have freed yourself from suffering and achieved enlightenment? Do you become a demigod infused with great power? Are you able to leap tall buildings in a single bound? Are you freed from all karma?

The short answer to all of these questions is no. It just means you don't have to live in New Jersey anymore. Or if, for some strange reason I could not even begin to comprehend, you still wanted to live in New Jersey, it would no longer create any suffering in you. In other words, you continue to live your life and meet the ups and downs that come with it but are better equipped to maintain balance and equanimity no matter what comes along.

You learn to be absolutely appropriate in every situation because you are seeing deeply into what is actually manifesting, and you understand it is an impermanent manifestation. Therefore, unpleasant experiences do not bring you down so far and pleasant experiences don't make you quite so high. You see the beauty and the value of each and every moment. Life itself becomes very sweet and enjoyable.

What The Buddha Taught

This, in a nutshell, is what the Buddha taught.

Of course, he taught for 45 years after his enlightenment and said many things, but in essence what he said were either reiterations of the Four Noble Truths or some clarification of the nature of reality that would help deepen understanding of the same truths. He was focused like a laser on the idea of ending suffering.

What The Buddha Didn't Teach

As I said, the Buddha was focused like a laser on the topic of ending suffering. It was commonly believed that the Buddha had knowledge of all metaphysical realms and manifestations as well, and he does hint at this knowledge at times, or at least he does not deny having access to it. But whenever asked to expound on metaphysics he demurred strongly.

In one instance, a monk approached him and began questioning him about the nature of the gods and demigods, other realms, and where we go after we die. He questioned the Buddha on all sorts of topics on the subject of metaphysics. The Buddha politely refused to answer his questions.

At some point the monk became frustrated, and told the Buddha that if he would not tell him these things, he, the monk, would have no choice but to leave the monastery. Still the Buddha refused and he gave this as an answer. "Monk, when you came to me did I promise you that I would teach you these things?" The monk agreed that the Buddha had made no such promise.

"You are like a person who has a poisoned arrow in them and I am the physician who is trying to heal you. You insist that you will not let me pull the arrow out until I have described for you the exact construction of the arrow, what type of feathers make up its fletching, what is the head composed of, what type of wood the shaft is made of. I tell you that by the time I had answered all of your questions you would be dead. The things you ask are unimportant in the context of achieving liberation and would only prolong your suffering."

Thus the Buddha made abundantly clear that he was interested in teaching only one thing, and that focus on the metaphysical aspects of reality were nothing but another distraction. Therefore he refused to teach or talk about it. This is as interesting and instructive as the things he did talk about.

In Buddhism, there is no deity, nor any supernatural occurrences or miracles upon which we must invest faith in order to accept the validity of the teachings. Though in some of the later stories about the Buddha some embellishments are added to make him appear more than a man, the Buddha was very clear on this point as he told his followers not to try to perform any miracles because that would detract as well from the message of what was of paramount importance.

Significantly, there are no denials of metaphysics or life after death or reincarnation. In fact a reading of the Buddha's words does supply some hints as to the afterlife and reincarnation (dealt with in a later chapter), but these things that he said were in the context of ending suffering.

There is a clear and concise ordering of the importance or lack thereof of this knowledge. It is this lack of dogma and metaphysical belief set that cause many to question whether Buddhism is a religion or just a philosophy. For me the lack of dogma was what drew me to Buddhism in the first place. As for my opinion on whether Buddhism is a religion or a philosophy my answer is absolutely yes, it is.

CHAPTER THREE

Important Buddhist Concepts

The Proud Cloud

Once there was a little puffy white cumulus nimbus cloud that was floating freely in the sky and looking down at all of the natural beauty below him. One day he happened upon a clear and very still mountain lake whose surface was as smooth and reflective as the surface of a mirror.

For the first time he beheld his own image and was instantly in love. He decided that he was the most beautiful thing he had ever seen and that it would be a good thing if there was more to him. So he sucked up all of the moisture from the lake below and grew to three times his original size.

He was curious to see how he looked now so he went to another mountain lake and was awestruck at how his magnificence had grown with his size. He sucked up all the moisture from that lake as well and continued to do so whenever he came across a lake.

Soon he was so big that he realized the lakes were not enough for him. He ventured out over the ocean and began to draw all of the moisture into himself, growing bigger and darker until finally he was so big that he covered the entire world and blocked out the sun.

"I am the greatest of all creation," he thought. "I can even conquer the mighty sun."

At this point, due to his covering the sun, the temperature on the earth began to plummet. He was so heavy with moisture that as soon as the cold air touched him he began to rain. At first the rain came down as a drizzle, but before long it became a torrential downpour that was seemingly without end.

He rained and rained for several days and try as he might to suck up more moisture from the ocean, his blockage of the sun had so lowered the temperature that the water could not form into vapor. So he shrank and shrank until all that was left of him was a little wisp of a cloud and then, poof, he was gone. The sun shined down and the world went on as though nothing had happened.

Dharma

According to the Buddha, all the dharmas are empty. That is a profound statement and would probably be more effective if you understand what the heck a dharma is and what the Buddha means by saying that it is empty.

Dharma is a word that is central to Buddhism and Hinduism as well. In Buddhism it is one of the three refuges that Buddha talked about - those being, the Buddha, the Dharma and the Sangha. One takes refuge in the Buddha by seeking to become what the Buddha was and understanding that this is our true nature to do so. The Sangha means seeking the support of a like-minded community that is involved in walking the same path that you walk. As for the Dharma, there are basically three uses of the word. In the Hindu religion it refers to the set of laws and rules that you follow as a Hindu.

In Buddhism it has very different meaning though there is some relation. The Dharma in Buddhism encompasses the True nature of reality, whereas when it references things and objects that manifest, it is used in its less universal meaning.

For example, if I say that love and compassion are the way of the Dharma, I am using the first meaning. If I refer to a tree as a dharma, I am using the second meaning. Basically, the Dharma, when spoken of in the context of one of the three refuges, refers to the full body of manifestations in the universe and the truth about the actual nature of all manifestations. It is also used to describe the whole of the Buddha's teaching.

What it says basically is that everything that manifests has the same nature as all other manifestations. Absolutely anything you encounter in the universe is a manifestation of form that is made up of a combination of conditions that allow whatever it is to manifest. Therefore, a dharma can refer to one of these manifestations but is also meant to include the universal nature of all things as well. Clear? Don't worry it'll get clearer as we go on.

For example, a wooden table is a dharma but not just the manifestation of the wooden table. It is a dharma in the sense that you understand it contains a universal truth about all manifestations. A table is surely a table but it has that form of manifestation due to an infinite amount of non-table elements that go into allowing it to exist in the first place. This statement is true for all manifestations, humans included.

In the case of the table, the word dharma would refer to an object that contains the Dharma that says that all things are interrelated with everything else. A table is not just a table. It is a manifestation that arises as a result of many different factors that you would normally not think of when thinking of a table. A table is made of wood. Wood comes from trees. Trees require Sunlight and rain and earth and air without which it cannot manifest. In order for there to be these elements you would have to be on a world in which the conditions are right to support atmosphere and the right intensity of sunlight and the right amount of rain and earth with sufficient nutrients to let the tree grow. This has to do with the position of the planet relative to the rest of the solar system, that is dependent on the configuration of the galaxy, that itself is dependent on the makeup of the universe that began several billion years ago in the big bang. You get the idea.

Who and what we are is a combination of an infinite amount of factors and conditions that on the surface do not appear to have anything to do with who and what we are.

Going back to the table, were I to list all the conditions that have an impact on the manifestation of the table, I would have a list that never ended. The point is that all things that manifest are inextricably dependent on everything else. This is what is meant by the Buddhist idea of being one with everything.

But looking deeper we can see that absolutely everything is needed in order for a table to exist. The tree itself is a manifestation of a living creature that has evolved over billions of years and has been able to do so because of everything that has happened in the history of the universe. Were there no big bang, were there no force of gravity, were there no chemical and physical laws which formed the planets and heavenly bodies including the earth, were there no formation of an atmosphere, were there no primordial biological soup, were there no single-celled organisms, were there no evolutional pressure and processes, were there no higher forms of life, were there no vegetation and finally were there no trees, there would be no table. Therefore the table's existence is due to all conditions that have occurred since the beginning of the universe.

Now realize that the same list applies to all of the conditions and manifestations contained in that list and you begin to glimpse the interconnectedness and interdependence of all things.

In short, that is the Dharma. It is the shorthand word for the true nature of all things as well as all of the manifestations of that nature.

This interconnectedness and interrelatedness of all things is contained in everything that exists. The Buddha called it Dependent Co-Arising or Dependent Origination.

The Law of Dependent Co-Arising

As I have said, a wooden table is a manifestation. It is made of wood. Wood is made up of elements of earth (trees), water (without which the tree could not be), air (without which the tree could not be), fire (specifically the sun, without which the tree could not be), and an infinite amount of other conditions all of which contribute to the ability to manifest a table.

Therefore, when we talk about a "table," we are using a type of shorthand to describe something that if we listed all the conditions that are part of what allows the table to be a table would take an infinite amount of time to relate. So we use a type of shorthand and call a table a table. Remove one element or change one condition and the table would no longer be a table.

This is the idea of Dependent Co-Arising. It is the idea that nothing exists as a separate manifestation from all other manifestations. As long as all the elements remain in a state that supports the existence of the table, the table can arise as a manifestation. When any of these conditions change, as they inevitably do, the table ceases to manifest as a table.

This simple truth seems strange to us because we are used to looking at things in shorthand. When I see a table I classify it as a table and look no deeper than that. If I look at the table mindfully, however, I begin to see all of the conditions that allow for the manifestation of the table and then I see the law of dependent co-arising, which shows me that the entire universe is in that table and in everything else.

Closely related to the concept of Dependent Co-Arising is the concept of Interdependence. It is the thought that all things cannot exist without the presence of every other thing.

It is the iteration of the Butterfly Effect. This thought experiment says that if a butterfly on the other side of the world flaps its wings, it could start a chain of events that lead to the end of the world. This is perhaps an overstatement of interdependence but it captures the spirit of the idea.

Another example of this is a match. You may think that if I strike a match on the flint that it will light. You would be right, but only if all of the conditions were present. Suppose you are in an environment with no oxygen. That match will never light no matter how hard you strike it. This is interdependence.

Impermanence

So with the acceptance of Dependent Co-Arising and Interdependence, we can see that all the things that we think of as solid and permanent are nothing of the sort. In fact, everything is composed of ever-changing conditions; therefore there is nothing that is solid and permanent.

To the contrary, we can say that everything is in a constant state of change and flux. The only unchangeable thing in the world is Buddha Nature. This is a central and very important concept in Buddhism. Learning to look upon everything as impermanent goes a long way in beginning to understand the origins of pain and suffering.

Because of the relatively short lives we lead in relation to things like mountains and other geological and evolutionary processes, we tend to look at manifestation of these processes as permanent since we cannot really perceive the slow, constant change that is taking place. Unless we happen to be at the end of a very long process in which one of these things reaches critical mass and change occurs relatively swiftly, we tend to think of these things as permanent.

This explains why so many people have a hard time wrapping their brains around the idea of climate change. Everyone thinks of climate as one of those things which is permanent and even when confronted with radical changes such as an increase in the frequency and intensity of certain weather events, the changes happen slowly enough that it is possible to maintain the illusion of permanence. Of course, this denial increases the amount of suffering when we are not prepared for what is occurring and will inevitably lead to greater suffering in the future.

The impermanent nature of the universe allows us to have appropriate connections with the world around us. If you are aware that anything manifesting in your life that is pleasurable is fleeting, you will learn to appreciate it fully while it is present and will not cling to it when it is past. Conversely, we do not fear unpleasant manifestations, as we understand that they are not permanent. It makes it much easier to pass through hard times.

Being aware of what causes suffering and seeing deeply into the nature of all manifestations leads to the understanding that suffering is a self-created condition.

No Self

If I turn my consciousness around and look at myself, I can see how Dependent Co-Arising and Impermanence support the idea of No Self. I, or what I short-handedly refer to as "I," am a collection of many conditions and elements. I am an aggregate of things that are not really an "I" at all.

I am beliefs and desires and perspectives and habits and fears and misconceptions grounded in ignorance, all of which go into creating the illusion that there is an actual unified thing here that I can call a self. But all of these things are subject to change. Therefore, unless I am making a statement about myself that is confined only to the present moment, anything I say or think of myself is absolutely untrue.

For example, what is your name? Can you say it? I am sure when you read this you are thinking that you know what your name is. My name is Marshall, middle name Charles (don't snicker!), last name Stern. Those are my names. When asked who I am I reflexively offer my first name or all three of them, depending on the context and who is asking. But what is a name?

If we look a little deeper, the correct answer to this question is that a name is nothing but a social contract. Rather than listing all of the things I believe make myself unique and which make me "me," we agree that this short-cut, this series of sounds, will stand for the collection of self-defining ideas and symbolize me.

What we have is a habitualized response to a question that in the ultimate sense is meaningless. Who am I?

Again, what I can say is that I have an agreement with the rest of society that I am accepting the convention that allows for us to use very truncated shorthand to refer to what we can generally consider to be my self. We live under an agreement that I shall be referred to by a certain collection of sounds that if approximated closely enough will result in my responding as though you are referring to what I consider to be me. What was your name before your parents picked one and had it written on your birth certificate? What name were you actually born with?

I am not "Marshall." There is nothing that connects that series of sounds to me other than the social agreement that over time has become so habituated and reflexive that I do not even question it anymore. I take it for granted that I am Marshall. I have identified with that sound.

Now, depending on how that sound is used in conjunction with other sounds or symbols or movements, I identify those things as referring to me as well. If someone makes a collection of sounds that I recognize as being derogatory that includes this name, I can feel wounded and wronged. Conversely, other sounds can make me feel joyous and prideful. With the unconscious acceptance of this one idea, I now personalize everything and view every thing through the lens of this construct called self. But, just as with my name, if you look deeply at this it becomes clear that there is no self there to be harmed or praised.

It is important to remember that when the Buddha said there is no self, no soul, and no separate existence that this is what he meant. Not that we do not exist, but that we exist in partnership with everything else. In fact, the Buddha never said there is no self. What he actually said is that there is no permanent separate self.

For example I may think of myself as a "happy" person. What does this mean? Am I always happy?

Nobody is always happy therefore the statement is meaningless. I may have a bad day and think of myself as unattractive but then a pretty woman flirts with me and I revise my self-definition. The point is that "I" is always changing, therefore there is no permanent "I." There is only a highly changeable set of factors that we mistakenly think of as an "I." Like everything else, what I think of as self is dependent on other conditions.

The fact is, as with all other manifestations, I do not actually have a separate "self" in the true sense of the word. Without everything else, there would be no me to begin with. I am everything, therefore I am no one thing. The manifestation of "I" is dependent upon the rest of the universe and everything and everyone in it.

So all things or dharmas are empty. This is a central concept of Buddhism. It means that if you look deeply enough at anything you will find it has no permanent separate self. In other words there is nothing that can be pointed to and about which it can be truly stated, "That thing is that thing and nothing else ever. If everything else passed away, that thing would still exist just as it is."

The fact is "that thing" only exists within certain conditions, which must be met in order for it to exist in the first place. It, like everything, is like a giant Jenga sculpture that remains stable only as long as none of the supporting blocks are moved. But if one is moved, the whole sculpture collapses.

This is not an easy concept to grasp, but in looking deeply at things, one can begin to see the universality of this truth. The practical application of this truth applies when we begin to turn our consciousness inward through the lens of impermanence, dependent co-arising and emptiness of self. Sooner or later we reach the realization that if all manifestations are merely aggregates of many different elements which are all empty of self, how can we be said to be anything but empty of self as well? That's when it starts getting interesting and herein lies the key to freedom.

A Case Of Mistaken Identity

You may be thinking at this point that this is all well and good but what does it have to do with suffering? It can be truly said that all suffering arises out of a universal case of mistaken identity.

In the previous chapters I said some unkind things about New Jersey. Let me tell you how I really feel about the Garden State. It is true that I am a native New Yorker and New Yorkers do tend to look down on New Jersey. That is where the humor comes from.

But I used to be a Boy Scout and my troop would hike a trail that went along the Palisades. If you've never seen them, they are beautiful cliffs only on the Jersey side of the Hudson River with miles and miles of wilderness trail. It is absolutely beautiful. I have many happy memories of that trail.

As a musician I played lots of gigs in New Jersey and got to see some of the best parts of the State. The Jersey

Shore was one of my favorites. What a wonderful area with gorgeous old hotels and boating and beaches. I was always happy to get a gig on the Jersey Shore.

Then there is the Delaware Water Gap that forms the boundary between New Jersey and Pennsylvania. It is a breathtaking vista of mountains and forests.

So by now you must be thinking, "Hey what's the deal? I thought this guy hated New Jersey. What I am writing now seems to directly contradict what I said before. So which is the Truth. Is Jersey a paradise or a fiery pit of yuck?

The answer is, both and neither. This poor little example was designed to illustrate the whole issue of identity and how it causes us to suffer. The fact is there is no such thing as New Jersey. All there is are lines drawn on a scaled down representation of the actual geography and labeled "New Jersey." New Jersey exists only in our minds and yet if you are from New Jersey you probably felt badly when I compared Jersey to hell, but felt proud when I proclaimed its virtues. You live in New Jersey therefore you identify with it as though it were a part of who you are.

This is how we get into trouble and cause ourselves to suffer. We mistakenly take all sorts of things like a job, marriage, children or schooling to determine who we are. When you first meet someone the first thing you do is to exchange names. The second thing you do is ask "what do you do?" The third thing is to get out pictures of the kids and grandkids. What you are doing is akin to drawing Jersey on a map. You say this is who I am when in fact you are revealing nothing about who and what you really are.

This sort of self-identification with things and names and labels creates a sense of insecurity since all of these things are subject to change. You may lose your job or lose a member of your family or get divorced. It is our job then to transcend this false identification so that we can then discover who we really are.

Buddha Nature

So who are we really?

All things or dharmas are empty. This is a central concept of Buddhism. It means that if you look deeply enough at anything you will find it has no separate self. In other words, there is nothing that can be pointed to and about which it can be truly stated, "That thing is that thing and nothing else. If everything else passed away, that thing would still exist."

The fact is "that thing" only exists within certain conditions, which must be met in order for it to exist in the first place. It, like everything, is like a giant game of Pick-Up Stix wherein you must be very careful not to move any other stix other than the one you are aiming for. But if one other is moved, you lose and the fact is that in this game all of the stixs are constantly moving.

It is easy to become confused by the doctrine of no self, and extend it inappropriately to the idea that since there is no self, we do not exist. There is a lot of confusion around this even by many Buddhists. But Buddhism is not nihilism.

There is a self, just not the one you think it is. For want of a better word we can call this self Buddha Nature. Remember the Buddha worked to free himself of suffering, to achieve enlightenment, and became the Buddha. He was not a god or a supernatural being. He was a man. The path he walked is the path we all must walk and it is the path that leads us home to our true self. It is the fully enlightened Buddha that is at the core of what we are.

In fact, we can say that acting in accordance with this, our own true nature brings us joy and equanimity, whereas acting against this nature brings us suffering. The Noble Eightfold Path is all about acting within Buddha Nature.

In the Tao it says the name that can be named is not the eternal name. This paradoxical statement applies to the self as well. The self that can be reduced for definition is not the eternal self. Buddha Nature, or the inherent divinity of all of mankind, exists. It just cannot be reduced to mental constructs or words.

So our True Nature is the only thing that is not subject to Dependent Co-Arising, No Self and Impermanence.

CHAPTER FOUR

Suffering is Optional

The Injured Boy

Once there was a boy who had skinned his knee playing with his friends. The wound hurt but not too badly. Still, he knew he had to treat it. One friend offered him an antiseptic, which he said would burn and intensify the pain for a short while, but after that the cut would heal faster and feel better.

His other friend offered him an ointment that numbed the area around the wound and took away the pain immediately but did nothing to promote healing. In fact, he would have to reapply it every so often to deaden the pain, and he cautioned that could lead to an infection over time. Now this young boy was very wise and so chose the antiseptic. He experienced the brief intense pain but after a few moments the pain subsided and he was as good as new. He and his friends went back to playing.

Sadness vs. Suffering

Right off the bat I want to reiterate the distinction between sadness and suffering. Sadness is an emotional process that allows us to move through grief and loss in a constructive way, leading though the pain of loss to the release of acceptance. Suffering is an add-on to organic sadness and can last as long as we continue to support the conditions that create it in the first place. It's the sensation of stopping the process of grieving by not accepting what is, leading perhaps to temporary relief but prolonging the period of suffering.

Sadness

When we begin to understand the Law of Impermanence, we see that loss is a continual and ubiquitous experience that makes the experience of sadness inevitable. As you live, you become attached to people and jobs and even objects. Remember, it is significant that the word motion forms the majority of the word emotion. It implies that the natural reaction to any experience is to allow a dynamic process to occur that is felt as a movement which leads through discomfort and finally ends in release. In order to experience the release that happens universally in all situations we must be willing go through the experience and not try to navigate around it.

Release is a wonderful feeling that is synonymous with freedom and cleansing. Sadness is not, as many of us are acculturated to believe, a negative emotion. It is a natural and organic method by which our hearts are refreshed and renewed. That's why it's called a good cry. Anyone who has had the experience of finally breaking down and crying after trying to be "strong" knows how good it can feel. It's like a rain shower that transforms a hot and humid day.

Sadness is inevitable if you are a sentient being. This is not bad news. Sadness doesn't hurt.

Suffering

Suffering, on the other hand, hurts like an S.O.B.

Suffering is what arises in our experience when we do not allow natural organic processes to complete. It is the sensation of the tension created as we try to hold back the inevitable turning of the wheel. By clinging to things as they are, or avoiding things as they are, we create a pale reflection of reality in which everything we experience is unsatisfying.

The acts of clinging or avoidance that cause our minds to wander into scary nightmare-like unconscious states are the root of dissatisfaction, which in turn causes the suffering. In fact, nightmares arise when we do not pay heed to our dreams. The longer we delay in listening to our higher self, the more insistent, scary and intense the dreams become.

The Law of Impermanence is central to understanding suffering in how it arises and what we can do about it. The ignorance of impermanence causes us to attach to things and experience continual loss, as the things we expect to be permanent disappear or change.

Nowhere is this more prevalent and intense than in our interpersonal relationships. We have libraries filled with literature about the subject of romantic love that always seems to fail in its promise to be eternal. Almost all of our music is likewise devoted to the idea that love will last forever, but somehow our hearts get broken because it doesn't. That is what makes the experience of pain inevitable. It's not very romantic to say, "I will be with you for as long as conditions allow," but that is the Truth.

To make matters worse, suffering remains with us in one form or another until we release our hold on the processes and allow them to complete. Unfortunately, to deal with suffering many of us turn to forms of relief that may alleviate the symptoms but that, in the end, fail to end the suffering and only intensify it, leading to the need for greater relief. This is the cycle of addiction.

We all suffer from addiction to one extent or another. In this sense, addiction includes but is not limited to the idea of drugs. There are many forms of relief, most of which take the form of distractions. Any tactic that keeps you from being present and facing what is real and frightening will offer some form of relief. You can settle for relief or you can go for release. Release is a true completion of the process, freeing you from it.

Relief and release are mutually exclusive. Release is the way of liberation and freedom. Relief is the way of strengthening self-imposed prisons. We must desire release to such an extent that we will not settle for mere relief. The end of suffering and the experience of release involve acceptance of what is. Relief supports denying what is and supports further suffering. In that sense we are all like the little boy who was offered the ointment that would ease his discomfort or the one that though it would hurt, would lead to actual healing. The choice is obvious.

This brings us back to desire. What we desire is what we move toward. The Buddha cautions us to overcome our desires in order to end suffering. This does not mean we cease to desire. Instead, it means we should train ourselves to rule our desire rather than allowing our desires to rule us.

When we become mindful and skillful with our desires, we can return to living in the real world of what is and in perfect harmony with our True Nature.

The Yin/Yang

Yin/Yang Wheel

I'm sure you have seen the Yin Yang symbol. As you can see, it is made up of two distinct and opposite sides each with a seed of the opposite within the opposing half. The Yin Yang should be seen as a wheel that is always turning. It is usually rendered as a static representation, but in fact is never static. This dynamic characteristic is important when trying to explain the nature of reality and why suffering is created.

The first thing we learn from the Yin Yang is that we have an illusion about the dual nature of reality. We think that there are such things as separate opposing forces that can exist independently. Everything is thought of in terms of polar opposites. Good or bad, up or down, in or out, high or low, black or white.

In fact, if you look a little deeper you will see that all of these pairs of opposites are not separate at all but exist as one whole concept. What does up mean without down?

Or in without out. We cannot have good without bad. The word is meaningless without its opposite partner for comparison. Our desire to have good win over bad is one example of this delusion so many of us share. The fact is, as we can plainly see by looking at the Yin Yang symbol, there can be no Good without Bad. Furthermore there is no such thing as pure Good or pure Bad. The seed of each pole is present within the essence of the other.

Think of black and white. If you had only black you would be blind. But if you had only white, you would be just as blind. It is the contrast between the two poles that gives meaning.

Things have meaning and form because of contrast. Without contrast there is nothing. This is what the Buddha means when he talks about dependent co-arising. All things are not separate permanent selves but interdependent conditions that arise and fall. The wheel is always spinning so nothing is static. This is impermanence and why change is inevitable and constant.

All things that exist are conditional and dependent on the manifestation of all other things. As conditions change, each manifestation changes. And conditions are always changing.

This wheel also illustrates the existence of impermanence. Because everything, as shown by the wheel of Yin Yang (Dharma), is seen to be in constant motion changing from one state to another, the very nature of reality is such that nothing that manifests lasts from one moment to the next in the exact same form. Everything is in a constant state of flux, arising and ceasing all the time.

If the nature of reality is such that there is nothing permanent because everything is dependent upon everything else and everything is always changing, it is then easy to see what causes suffering. To put it simply, if in ignorance of impermanence you set your heart on things which have no permanent manifestation, unless you learn this lesson, suffering will arise. You can buy all the insurance you can afford and all the locks and alarm systems that can be had, put all your valuables in a theft-proof vault, yet no matter what you do, in the end you will lose everything but your True Self.

To take the illustration even further, imagine that our lives are spent standing next to the wheel and watching it spin. When the wheel is in one position perhaps we experience something wonderful, but as it spins we may experience something painful. This is still living in the moment and being present with what is manifesting at the time so we are doing okay. Where we get into trouble is when we decide either that pleasant time was so pleasant we want it to last forever, or that painful time was so painful we never want to experience it again. We then try all sorts of strategies that are doomed to failure.

We can try to hold the wheel in place, to keep it from spinning, but since the motivating force of the wheel comes from universal law, we are never strong enough to accomplish this.

We might also try running to keep up with the spinning of the wheel, which we may be able to do for a while but sooner or later we are going to become very tired, dizzy and fall down. We can either cling to a portion of the wheel or try to avoid a portion of the wheel. For the vast majority of us, that is how we live our lives and that is why suffering is so prevalent. The attempt to control dynamic forces of change that cannot be controlled gives rise to tension between the True force of nature and us. The friction it creates forms the sensation of suffering.

We Do It To Ourselves

The wheel will continue to spin at its own pace and there is nothing we can do to change that. If you cannot accept that truth you are in for a rough time.

This is what the Buddha tried to tell us. We cause our own suffering mostly through ignorance of these simple truths concerning the True nature of what we are and what the universe is about. We live lives of constant striving to achieve things that are doomed from the start. The suffering is not inherent in the universe; it is artificially created by our own actions. The need for security in an inherently insecure universe is a Sisyphean task, eternal and futile.

The ancient myth of Sisyphus concerns a man condemned by the gods to roll a heavy boulder up a hill but every time he nears the crest it rolls back down again. This eternal and futile task represents the futility of trying to control that which is beyond your control.

Hence the serenity prayer: Lord grant me the serenity to accept the things I cannot change, the courage to change the things I can and the wisdom to know the difference.

You can resist the turning of the wheel only so long until the resistance grows too great and it rolls out of your grasp. At that time you can learn the lesson and stop repeating this futile act, or you can start all over again trying to stop the turning of the wheel and live through yet another cycle of suffering.

In other words, you can fight what is because you can't accept it or you can learn to accept whatever is and make peace with the fact that you can't prevent change from happening. It is the difference between creating suffering and living in peace and contentment.

The Way Out Of Suffering

So if clinging and avoiding due to ignorance were the causes that lead to suffering, it would seem a simple matter to end suffering. All you need do is simply stop clinging and avoiding through educating yourself as to the True Nature of the Universe. Problem solved. You are healed and can now live the rest of your life without suffering. Thank you for coming and don't forget to tip your waitress.

What's that you say? How do you change deeply ingrained habits and unconscious reflexive behaviors so that you can stop clinging and avoiding? Well, if you want to know that you had better sit back down. This is going to take a while, and some hard work on your part.

Remember that just because something is simple, and the answer here is very simple, that does not mean it is easy to achieve. What does it mean not to cling? It means practicing non-attachment. The idea of how to end suffering is very simple but in no way is it easy.

Imagine you had to say goodbye to everyone you know and everything you own and journey to a place very distant, where nobody knows you and where the culture is so different from your own that you are going to feel utterly lost and alone. In addition, nobody speaks English so communication is going to be a problem. Sound absurd? It is actually inevitable that we lose all that we hold dear if what we hold dear is impermanent. This may seem cruel unless you understand that everything we hold dear keeps us from recognizing who and what we really are and keeps us living in ignorance and suffering. Loss is a great teacher.

This is the premise of the great Frank Capra film "It's A Wonderful Life." George Bailey, the main character, after a great deal of suffering meets his guardian angel who grants him the wish that he'd never been born. George goes to places and people he had known before, sees how much is changed, and comes to realize he has lost everything. He is terrified, prays to live again and the wish is granted. This is what we are all in for. Absolutely everything that we use to identify ourselves is, sooner or later taken from us.

The fact is that everything I mentioned in that list above will sooner or later come to pass. By clinging to "possessions," including relationships and ways of seeing yourself, you are ripe for suffering as each one of these things passes from the state of earthly manifestation. In our society there are whole industries based upon feeding your fear and enabling you to have the illusion of security as though you could prevent loss. You can arm yourself to the teeth and install the most sophisticated alarm systems and lock yourself in a Panic Room Vault, buy the most comprehensive insurance policies in the world, but none of that will slow by one second the inevitable loss of everything you hold dear. Even your own body will eventually fail.

Now, before you throw yourself out of a window from reading all of this "good news," let me explain why this is, indeed, good news.

Remember what I said before? Not one of these things we think we must have to live is actually necessary for our continued and fully-functional joyful living. Everything we attach to is like a drug that buffers us from feeling the full impact of life as a dynamic force. Much of what we hold on to, we do out of fear - fear of something like the vision I painted above. Though loss is a great teacher, sometimes the greatest teachers are the ones we fear and avoid the most. Think about how in Dickens' *A Christmas Carol*, Scrooge reacts to the spirits who haunt him and yet it is that very experience that saves him and transforms him from a miserable old miser into a man of love and compassion. We are all

Scrooge learning to love again. The challenges we face in life are the Spirits.

We hold on out of fear, and avoid out of fear, but fear is a very bad teacher and an even worse guide to living a fulfilled and actualized life. It is not in our true nature to fear and anything we do that goes against our True nature causes us suffering.

Even worse, when we begin to listen and obey fear we become slaves to it. It whispers in our ears that only by doing what it tells us to do are we ever truly safe. It sends us on a never-ending scavenger hunt for security. Security is something we think we can achieve but in fact nobody ever has. It is another futile eternal task, like Sisyphus rolling the rock up the hill.

Modern nations, the United States chief among them, have stored arsenals and military capabilities with power to destroy all living things on earth multiple times. Yet we are still so insecure that our people starve while billions are poured into more new weapons. We can't seem to pass sensible gun safety measures because a large enough portion of our fellow citizens are so afraid that they think a gun will protect them.

The alternative to this is learning to let go of what you think you "need" and to learn to be content with what you have in the present moment. You will find if you live this way, you always have what you need to live a joyful life.

In living this way, you transform from acting like a frightened child hiding under the table to a free human being walking unfettered in the sun. This equanimity is the goal of Buddhists who wish to be free. It requires a bone deep trust that comes from wisdom, secure in the knowledge that the universe we inhabit is a system based upon and suffused with perfect compassion and unconditional love.

When this Truth inhabits your heart you begin to see endings in a very different light. You still experience sadness at the passing of that which you love, but there is also a sense of excitement over what is coming to take its place.

It is important to note that non-attachment does not mean that you remain aloof and unattached from everything around you. Un-attachment and non-attachment are not the same.

To the contrary, to be non-attached means you can fully attach in the present moment because you are not attached to the past. You can love who is before you because you have accepted the loss of a previous love that is no longer present. If you cannot be trusting enough to let that past relationship go when the time comes for separation, you will not be present for this new love that has found you. If your heart is full of longing there is no room to fill it with love.

The whole idea of non-attachment is one of the most misunderstood ideas of Buddhism. For this reason I will present a short fable that I have written to illustrate the idea behind attachment and non-attachment.

Screwdriver Man

Once, a long time ago, in an age before there was any differentiation between people, a time where everyone wore baggy white jump suits with close fitting white hoods, an unnamed man was walking along enjoying the scenery.

All of a sudden he saw something sticking out of one of the walls of a nearby house. He saw that this could be a danger to any unwary traveler and so he determined to fix the problem. On closer inspection he saw that it was a screw. He had never seen a screw before but somehow he knew what it was.

He looked around for anything that might help him and there lying on the ground right under the screw was a screwdriver. He assumed that was the solution to this problem. He picked it up and tried several unsuccessful attempts at using the tool to fix the issue. He tried banging the screw in with the blunt end of the handle. No go. He tried waving the screwdriver like a wand and commanding the screw to right itself. Other than a sore throat from yelling commands it had no effect. Finally he looked closer at the screw and noticed a notch cut into the head. Being a bright fellow, he compared the notch on the screw with the blade of the screwdriver. It didn't take him too long after that to find the proper application of this new tool.

While he was struggling to find the solution, a crowd of people had gathered unbeknownst to him to watch him work out the problem. When he finally applied the tool in the right way everyone applauded and cheered loudly for the man. That made him feel very good. No one had ever stood out for anything before this. He was just about to put down the screwdriver and continue on his way when a thought stopped him. This tool came in very handy and seemed to be the cause of the adulation of his fellow townsfolk. Perhaps he should hold on to it just in case.

Sure enough, he came upon another loose screw and dealt with it with confidence. Again the crowd ooohed and ahhhed. He started actually seeking out loose screws and soon became know for this. The people gave him a name. He was "Screw Driver Man." Now when he entered a village all the children would run to meet him yelling, "Here's Screw Driver Man, he's actually here!" Young available ladies were very interested in him. One enterprising young woman actually made him a leather holster for his screwdriver with the letters "SDM" embedded on the side in sequins.

Life went along smoothly and wonderfully for him until one day he experienced an existential crisis. He spied something sticking out of wall and walked up confidently, screwdriver in hand to address the problem. When he reached out to fit his screwdriver into the slot that every screw had, he could find no place to fit the blade. In fact, upon closer inspection he saw that this screw had no threads on the side. The thought came to him then that this was not a screw at all, but a nail.

He tried using his screwdriver to bang it in but to no avail. He happened to look down and there lying on the ground, was a hammer. The crowd grew restless. How would Screw Driver Man deal with this crisis? He considered putting down the screwdriver and picking up the hammer but he noticed the rapt attention of the crowd. "What will I be if I do this?" he thought, I'm Screw Driver Man not Hammer Man!" He walked away from the nail. From that point on he had made himself a limited human being who could only deal with one type of problem.

On a very simple level, non-attachment it is like working with tools. In order to use a screwdriver you must firmly attach your hand to it and grasp it. When you have tightened all the screws and must now bang in a nail, you must first detach from the screwdriver by putting it down and then attach and grasp a hammer. This is non-attachment. It is a manifestation of being present so that you can act appropriately for what is happening now. Non-attachment should not be confused with un-attachment. With non-attachment one detaches from things that are past and no longer appropriate so that they can fully attach to what is appropriate in the present moment. If your hands are full of baggage you are carrying from the past, you cannot accept the gifts that are given you in the present.

The Free

A person who has freed him or herself from suffering is said to have attained enlightenment. I think this is an unfortunate use of the word attainment and it has certainly led to a good deal of confusion. First of all, there is nothing to attain that you do not already have.

If you look at it more deeply, the word enlightenment implies something quite different than that, which is imagined by most. It is not uncommon to have the thought that one could never achieve enlightenment because it means being blissful all the time and rising above everything. How does one even begin doing that?

Enlightenment refers to the lightening of one's person by casting off the unnecessary burdens weighing them down and keeping them from seeing what they already know in their deepest hearts. It is the softening of your heart so that rather than living in a fortress protecting yourself from all manner of threats, you are free to travel life's roads and discover the wonders that await you. It is not a retreat from reality but a way of fully experiencing reality.

The process of enlightening oneself is actually a process of letting go, and as a result the enlightened person certainly becomes lighter. This lightening allows for one's true Buddha Nature to shine, as evidenced by the great compassion motivating everything they do. It also allows the person to be equanimous whatever the situation. They are content to allow the wheel to spin and readily accept what is.

This means they act appropriately in every situation because they are perfectly tuned in to what is extant in the moment, being non-attached to the past or the future. Therefore you see a person who experiences no friction or strain in his or her life. Their demeanor is very steady and calm no matter what the circumstance is. They radiate a calm aura wherever they are. They neither get too high nor too low but are very constant.

They practice what I call Radical Acceptance, meaning there is nothing that arises in their experience that they can't accept. I personally learned about radical acceptance while I was driving on the Long Island Expressway one afternoon in rush hour. Let me tell you about driving on the L.I.E. in rush hour. The L.I.E. is the main road between Manhattan and the eastern end of Long Island. Every morning the westbound traffic is appalling and every afternoon the eastbound traffic is...well let me put it this way, it is the cheapest parking you will ever find in New York.

As I was saying, one afternoon I was heading east on the Expressway and as per usual I was stuck in traffic. I was right around Douglaston Parkway in Queens, and the traffic came to a dead stop. People were getting out of their cars after several minutes of not moving at all. I was being a good New Yorker and going crazy with impatience while looking at my watch and feeling like I was in driving hell.

Then all of a sudden I looked out to my left and saw Douglaston Bay, the sailboats, the majestic Throggs Neck Bridge and the reclaimed wetlands while the warm sun caressed my face. A phrase occurred to me: "I can accept this." At that precise moment all of my tension melted away and a big smile bloomed on my face. That is Radical Acceptance - the ability to be okay no matter the situation.

This does not mean that you do not recognize when something is wrong and attempt to rectify it. On the contrary, Radical Acceptance simply means that you accept what is, in all of its aspects even in its wrongness. In seeing and experiencing this wrongness the enlightened person will act in an entirely appropriate manner to make what corrections are needed if they have the power to affect change, but it will not disturb their peace. Think of Ghandi.

A free person can experience a full range of emotions, from joy to sadness to love and even anger when it is appropriate in the situation. Most importantly, because they accept everything and allow every moment to be exactly what it already is, they experience no conflict with the world around them and do not experience suffering. They are truly free.

Where Can I Get Some Of That?

This is all well and good, but for most people it sounds like something that is beyond their reach. This person I have described hardly sounds human. Yet the one essential defining characteristic of the enlightened is that they are very human.

Enlightenment is not a destination you go to and remain forever without applying what the Buddha taught. Likewise, anyone following the path of the true Dharma will eventually find his or her way to this place and state of being. At first you will experience glimpses of enlightenment, moments of clarity and equanimity followed by periods of suffering and error followed again by longer and longer periods of enlightenment. How this happens is by applying the Noble Eightfold Path, and especially the last step of Right Concentration. All Buddhists who follow the Noble Eightfold Path spend time in meditation.

The Eighth Step

When you have developed right thinking and right ethics and are trying to live your life in a way that honors these steps, a strong practice of meditation enables and supports all of your efforts. The practice of meditation trains your mind to quiet and focus itself so that it can hear the still small voice of Truth - the Dharma - that is always present for everyone. This, of course, is the voice of our own Buddha Nature that is always present within us. In order to hear it we must learn to quiet ourselves. This is why we practice meditation.

CHAPTER FIVE

Meditation

The Inheritance

There was once a very poor young man who lived in the shabbiest hut in the village. One day there was a knock upon his door. When he opened it he was surprised to find a man dressed in fine clothing.

"You are the young man who lives here?" he asked.

When the young man affirmed that he was indeed the person who resided here, the finely dressed gentleman informed him that he was his uncle's lawyer and that he had tracked the young man down in order to give him his inheritance. His rich uncle had recently passed away and left his nephew his entire fortune. The only condition was that he would have to reside in his uncle's palace in a town two days walk away from here.

The young man excitedly said that he would do so immediately and couldn't believe his good fortune. The lawyer handed him a golden key and warned him not to lose it.

"If you do not move into your uncle's palace within three days, the entire fortune will be given to charity."

The very next day the young man gathered up what meager belongings he had and set out to walk to the town where his uncle's palace was located. On the second day, as he was only a few miles from there, he was stymied when the road crossed through a shallow river. The road dipped into the river and crossed it but the traffic going back and forth made it impossible for him to cross that way. So he decided to cross the river by walking through the fallen trees and bushes to the side of the road.

He made it through and finally arrived at the palace. His heart pounding in his chest he reached down for the key that he attached by string to his waistband and to his horror found that it was no longer there. He looked all over and could not find it.

Then he recalled crossing the river and how the branches of the downed trees and bushes pulled at him. "It must have fallen there," he thought. He made his way back to the river and began frantically looking for the lost key. It was probably in the water but because there was so much traffic the water was opaque with mud and stirred up sediment. He tried feeling around in the murky water but it was an impossible task.

He decided to sit and wait for the traffic to slow. After a while his patience was rewarded. As the traffic slowed and the water cleared he could see a golden object lying in the water. It was indeed the key. Through patience he had found his treasure.

Meditation is the practice of Radical Acceptance. We sit with whatever we find in our present situation and by accepting everything as a gift, we begin to see deeply into what is around us. We see clearly what we are clinging to and where we are avoiding, and relax the unconscious habitual impulses to do either. At least that is what we strive to do. It takes time and work to be able to accomplish this.

In meditation we do not seek to change anything but instead use this time to become still and silent enough so that we can truly become present with the present moment. We discover sensations in our bodies and the complementary reflexes we have developed and allowed to become unconscious through years of habit and repetition. We breathe in those situations where we feel impatience and suffering arise and rather than trying to fix the problem, by focusing on the breath, allow the processes to complete and reach acceptance at which point we can feel our body releasing stress and anxiety.

In meditation we experience an itch, for example, and feel the hand begin to move seemingly of its own accord to scratch. Notice this for yourself. An itch will arise. How hard is it to just sit and allow the itch to be what it is without interference on your part? While we are meditating and training ourselves in mindfulness, we do not allow the hand to move and we get to experience the full cycle of the itch from arising to its apogee and all the way through to its cessation. When we do this enough times, we begin to regain conscious control of this impulse to automatically react to discomfort.

Remember what I said about the value of those experiences we would rather avoid? Discomfort is big on that list of experiences. We carry around a whole collection of habituated behaviors and tactics for avoiding discomfort. These tactics have become reflexive and are no longer under conscious control. It's very difficult for someone who is new to meditation to sit perfectly still for any length of time without experiencing some form of discomfort and this triggers a habitual response.

Feel an itch? Your hand moves without thought to scratch it. Feel an ache? Your body moves to ease it. Feel tension? Your body tenses up to do something about it. These reactions are mostly automatic and it is the main purpose for new meditators to return those unconscious reactions to conscious control. The problem is not that you are uncomfortable and decide to do something about it. The problem is you find yourself doing it before you have had a chance to make a conscious decision.

In fact, there is a great deal of discomfort in meditation that one experiences, especially when beginning to practice. There are many occasions on which to learn this lesson and to begin to develop mastery over your mind, to wake up the sleepwalking self. Therefore, when beginning a meditation practice, be grateful for all the discomforts that manifest for you. Each one is an opportunity for you to regain control of your mind

What Is Meditation?

Meditation is the act of listening with your whole being. "Listening to what?" you may ask. Until we begin to sit and quiet our minds we are simply not aware of how much noise and chaos exists within our heads and hearts. We are like fish swimming in water, unaware that water exists because it is so ubiquitous it is simply taken for granted. Think about it. How often do you notice the air and atmosphere you are constantly interacting with and taking into your body?

Likewise, and especially in our current world, noise and overwhelming stimulus is the rule rather than the exception. For example, it is very rare nowadays to go into a business of any type and not find a television playing or music blaring. Even formerly quiet places such as restaurants have taken to constantly attacking our senses with a cacophony of sounds and other stimuli. We are constantly bombarded with messages telling us to buy something or want something.

The tactic used by the vast majority of these marketers is to elicit tension and fear in us. They appeal to our reflexive habitual reaction to discomfort to make us crave relief of the tension. Then they try to sell us something to relieve the discomfort. This makes us better consumers as we load ourselves up with all types of stuff we don't need.

The tension and fear that bombard us regularly become familiar. It has become what we consider to be normal on an unconscious level. Now letting it go becomes unthinkable. We learn to associate tension with the feeling of being alive. The noise and the bombardment are taken as everyday life and never questioned. There is an Italian restaurant in my neighborhood that serves delicious food in an authentic atmosphere while playing Italian love songs. Then they spoil it all by having a huge flat screen TV that is always tuned to Fox news.

Even more insidious is the fact that since people are so regularly bombarded with noise, there appears to be an actual fear of silence. I have had the experience on many occasions where I have been in a waiting room or a restaurant or some other establishment and requested that the music or television be turned off, and been met with a great deal of resistance and even hostility at the idea.

This resistance to silence is indicative of people and whole societies who are badly in need of meditation practice. There is so much wisdom available to all of us if we can get quiet enough to hear it. The key is being brave enough to let go of the constant stimulus long enough to allow yourself to bathe in a warm tub of silence and stillness.

However, becoming quiet does not require you to be on a lonely mountaintop. The quiet you are trying to experience is the quiet that exists inside of us. It is at the center of what we are. As we learn to sit and be quiet within ourselves, especially in the midst of chaos, we begin to experience true silence. I have meditated on jet planes, on subways, in waiting rooms, and at airport gates (most of which had CNN constantly playing) and had wonderful experiences doing so. Of course, it is certainly optimal to sit, especially when you first begin, in a quiet relatively chaos-free place. But if you don't have a choice, it is always better to sit than not to sit. Sitting with a difficult circumstance is synonymous with the idea of sitting with discomfort. Noise can be a source of serious discomfort. The ability to sit and be at peace in the midst of that noise is a very valuable skill to acquire.

You may even find when trying to sit that things arise to distract you from sitting. As soon as your butt hits the cushion your phone, that has been silent all day, suddenly starts to ring non-stop. Your neighbor has just purchased a new leaf blower and can't wait to use it. Your pets may decide this is the optimal moment to sit on your lap or beg to be fed.

In my case, I had a wonderful Black lab mix named Crow T. Dogbutt. (MST3K fans will get the reference. He looked just like the silhouette of Crow T. Robot). I had a futon in my zendo that was Crow's place to lie down while I meditated, which he always did when I sat. At one point Crow developed an annoying habit of slowly licking the futon loudly and persistently. At first I interrupted my sit to get him to stop. Then I realized that Crow was teaching me something. I was able to imagine how much I loved my weird dog and when it no longer annoyed me he stopped doing it.

Meditation is the profound act of listening to whatever is present. It is not spacing out and traveling to other dimensions. It is not about controlling anything; in fact it is all about letting go of the need to control everything. It is learning how to be joyfully rooted in the here and now.

What Meditation is Not

The idea of meditation is not new in the West but as with many aspects of Buddhism there are many myths and misunderstandings surrounding it.

One question that I hear from students is about what to do with the mind during meditation. "How do I make my mind completely blank so that I can meditate?" they ask.

The only way I am aware of to make the mind completely blank is through serious head trauma. I don't recommend it. In meditation we do not try to make anything be anything. To the contrary, we are learning to be at peace with what is. During some meditations your mind is noisy. If that's the case, sit with the noise. Sometimes your mind will be very calm and restful. That's nice too but the trick is not to get attached to those pleasant experiences. Noisy or calm, all meditation is beneficial. Below I will tell you what you can do to help quiet your mind in a skillful way.

Another one I hear is "I can't meditate, I have tried but I just can't do it." To that I respond that meditation is being with whatever is in the present moment. If while you are sitting quietly and all you are aware of is your mind saying over and over "I can't do this, I can't do this, I can't do this", congratulations, you have found your mantra. Let it be what it is. Given time and acceptance it will change. Remember Impermanence.

Or, "If I meditate regularly I'll become weird." I say this in my class and then ask the students the following, "I meditate regularly. Am I weird?" This gives every class without fail the opportunity to shout in unison "YES!" It is my gift to my students. Seriously though, you do not have to sell everything you own and sit on a mountaintop for twenty years dressed only in a diaper in order to have a regular meditation practice. On my radio show, I once interviewed Congressman Tim Ryan from Ohio who is a regular Meditator. You'd be surprised how many famous and successful people meditate regularly. Phil Jackson the former coach of the Chicago Bulls in their heyday is also a regular meditator.

This one I hear a lot, "There is a right way to meditate and I just don't know how to do it." Is there a right way to meditate? The answer is yes...and no. There is a right way to meditate but that right way is individual to you. You must, through trial and error, find out what that is for yourself. Anything that supports you in being still and silent is the right method for you. Please give any method you learn enough time to see if it's working for you. Three months should do it.

"I'll betray my own religious beliefs." The Congressman Tim Ryan I mentioned before is a devout Catholic. How does he meditate without betraying his religion? Simple. Every religion known to man has a form of meditation within it. If you are interested in meditation but you want to do it within the confines of your religion, go to your Rabbi, or Pastor or Imam and ask them how to do that.

So what are the practical results of meditation on the body?

The Body as an Instrument

All things that manifest in the universe vibrate at a certain frequency. This applies to our physical bodies as well. There is an optimal frequency at which we can operate, in which we experience peace and harmony. Unfortunately, few of us have found our optimal frequency.

In fact, as a guitarist I have had to learn the lesson of optimal frequencies. The optimal frequency for the A string is 440 hz in the West. All other strings have actual optimal frequencies as well. When they are stretched to vibrate at those exact frequencies, you get a pleasant harmony of musical notes. When one or all are out of tune, the whole instrument is very hard to listen to. It becomes discordant.

This is a great analogy for understanding the body. When the body is out of tune, which happens as a result of stress, it's just like strings that have been struck and stretched. The feel of the body is discordant and inharmonious. When it is in tune or attuned, the body functions in a perfect and harmonious fashion. Leaving the body out of tune will eventually lead to more chronic states. Just as an untuned guitar will develop neck problems, the body will suffer certain diseases as a result of being too tight or too loose.

Eastern medicine identifies centers of energy within the body called chakras. These centers of energy are seen to vibrate at various optimal frequencies. When they are vibrating at this optimum frequency, they are like any stringed instrument that is in tune. The effect is a beautiful sound. Bodies in tune are so much like a stringed instrument capable of playing beautiful music.

Siddhartha realized the Middle Way and saw it was the correct path. He thought of the lute he played as a young person, and how if the strings were too tight they broke and if too loose they made no sound at all.

Tuning the Body and Mind

Of course when I am speaking about the body I am including the mind as well, because everything starts and ends with the mind. It is actually the mind you are attuning that has an effect on the body.

Meditation is the act of retuning the mind and body to work in optimal frequency. What we are doing when we stay in silence and stillness is returning ourselves to our natural state. We are returning to the source of everything and allowing ourselves to vibrate at the frequency we would naturally vibrate if we never created stress or clung or grasped or avoided or experienced fear.

This is the frequency we naturally vibrate at. As with suffering, it is we ourselves who pull ourselves out of tune. You could even say that G-d is the guitarist and we are His instruments. When we meditate, we allow Him to put us back in tune.

Another analogy might be that of a road and the grass underneath it that yearns to grow. The road is built upon the earth and suppresses it with concrete and asphalt. If left alone, the earth would reclaim that spot. Grass would grow through the cracks in the surface, doing what comes naturally in reaching for the sun. The road would eventually disappear and be replaced with soil and grass. In order for the road to continue to be, someone must continually repair it and repave it.

In the same sense, if we stop paving over the places in us that yearn to be free, freedom will come to us. This is great news for the lazy among us (I was going to start a fan club for this but it was too much work.) The process of freeing ourselves is not one that involves effort or strain. It demands the opposite. It demands effortless effort, which in Chinese is called Wu Wei (pronounced: Woo Way).

It requires us to develop an ability to allow organic processes to play out without interfering or trying to control them. It is the ability to understand the Dharma and trust that the processes will always lead to the best possible outcomes.

Meditation retunes us and "works" when we are able to be still and do nothing. If we have an itch, we do not scratch. If we are experiencing minor pain, we breathe through it and let it be. We learn and train ourselves to be content with things as they are. We learn that if we do not interfere, everything is taken care of. The itch does not need to be scratched; it will follow a course on its own that will lead to its cessation. The small pain likewise will fade on its own without our intercession. When we learn that this is a universal truth and we start living our lives in this way, we stop clinging and avoiding.

We know that just like the itch, everything we love will appear, reach a crescendo and disappear on its own. We cannot change that. Of course this also means that when we experience something we don't like, we know fighting it or avoiding it are unnecessary since it will take care of itself. We become calmer and unafraid. We experience everything as just another experience.

Where we find strong emotions and attachment, we experience the cycle of arising and ceasing as an important lesson and learn not to attach beyond its time in the future. In short, we become free.

Meditation is the practical experience that makes this state of being possible. Along with the important lessons of the other seven steps of the Noble Eightfold Path, this is the one that encompasses all of the others. In meditation, you experience first hand the Truth of the Buddha's words. You get to live the Dharma. It is nothing but practical, thus Buddhists refer to meditation as their "practice."

What's the Right Way to Meditate?

Forgive me; I am going to put on my musician's hat for a bit in order to draw out this metaphor for "tuning" ourselves. If you are not a guitar player, you may not get what I am describing but I trust you can follow along anyway. In any case, I will return to Zen teacher mode shortly. (It's such a good metaphor that I cannot resist *amplifying* and adding to what I said earlier about guitar tuning.)

With a guitar, we use several methods to make sure the instrument is in tune. We can use a tuning fork, which gives us a tone to tune to. Once one string is in tune, we then tune the rest through relative tuning. We can find the relative tuning by holding down the fifth fret on the previous string (or fourth on the G string) and plucking the next string to make the tone identical, or we can use harmonics whereby we gently touch the string and pluck, inducing a very high and pure relative tone and then compare it with the next string. We listen for the oscillations and as they approach perfect tuning the oscillations will slow until there is no oscillation at all. Then it is in perfect tune.

Of course, we can tune the guitar by finding the notes on a piano or other instrument that we know is in tune, or we can use an electronic tuner where the lights and dials tell us when the string is in perfect pitch. We can even develop perfect pitch in ourselves and thereby become a human tuning machine. All of these methods will work and all of them are available to be used. There is no one right method for tuning a guitar.

Okay, musician hat off. That wasn't so bad was it?

You may be wondering about now why I am giving you a lesson in guitar string tuning in a book about Buddhism. Just as with tuning, there is no "right" way to meditate. We use meditation to allow us to restore ourselves to our perfect attunement but the way we choose to accomplish this is not proscribed.

To connect the guitar tuning metaphor to Meditation, just as tuning by comparing relative tones, we can learn to meditate by observing others and trying to pick up on their methods. As tuning with harmonics, which requires silence and careful listening, meditation also requires silence and careful listening as well as sensitivity to when things are conflicted and oscillating as opposed to when they are in perfect tune and there is no discord. Fine-tuning using the notes on a piano or other instrument is like finding a wise teacher who can help you find the right method for you because of their experience or using a guided meditation to get you started. All of these methods are valid, it's just a matter of finding out what works best for you.

For myself, I prefer sitting in Za Zen, which for me means sitting on a cushion in half lotus position, eyes slightly open and attending my breathing for two forty-five-minute periods a day. This is what works best for me.

Additionally, for longer meditations or where sitting is not practical, I may use walking meditation or Kinhin. As the name implies, I walk in a very slow and deliberate fashion but with one of my hands cupped over the other which is in a fist, left on top of right, and attending the process of walking and each individual step in a very deep way, as well as focusing on my breath. This is often used as a break from sitting meditation when you are sitting for a long period of time as in a monastery. It gets the blood flowing back to your legs that can go numb during long sits.

I have also done Yoga, conscious eating, and simple breathing as forms of meditation. However, the type of mediation that resonates best for me is the sitting in Za Zen with a mix of some Tibetan traditions and a good dose of insight meditation. Does that mean it is a superior form of meditation? Not at all, it's just what works best for me.

What I suggest is that you pick a form of meditation to start with and stick with it for three months. If this method is working for you, then great, stay with it. You have found an effective form of meditation for yourself. If not, seek another form or method. Don't be afraid to make changes and alterations that may work better for you. Some people love chanting after sitting, some prefer to remain silent. I know people who will spend one day a week in complete silence not uttering a word or a sound. It is a very profound experience if you have never tried it.

As I said, I sit in my own mix of Za Zen, insight meditation and some Tibetan techniques the majority of the time. In addition I also have my own rituals that work for me. I use a singing bowl which I strike three times to begin and twice to end. I let the tone ring until it is completely gone before striking again. I end each sit with a gasho bow - a bow accomplished with hands together in front, palm to palm as if in prayer. This is a sacred and respectful way of saying thank you and is just about universal in Asia. I bow to Buddha Nature, which is a bow out to the True Self that the Buddha found is in everyone, and a bow to anyone who happens to be sitting with me, including others who have been a part of my meditation without knowing it. This may include the guy on the leaf blower outside my window who has acted as a teacher for me in learning to sit and remain still no matter what. Other than that, my sitting is pretty pro forma. Feel fee to follow your heart in creating rituals that work for you in your mediation practice.

Gasho Bow

One Suggested Method To Begin

You have to start somewhere if you want to start meditating, and if by this point you don't yet want to, I suggest you go back and reread the book up to this point.

Since I am most familiar with Za Zen, I am going suggest this method to begin with. I strongly suggest you try it everyday at the same time in the same place, (preferably not in your bed or bedroom unless you have no choice as it could affect your sleep), and follow my instructions for the first three months. After three months, feel free to try other methods or make any alterations you feel would benefit your practice. The reason for this has to do with habituation. When you sit every day in the same way it becomes easier to do as you become habituated to the structure of your sitting. Changing too often can interrupt this process.

Zendo

A "zendo" is a room or space that is specifically used for the purpose of sitting in meditation. The cushion we sit on in Za Zen is called a zafu and the mat that it goes upon is called a zabutan. If you would like to use these things to aid your meditation they are available online. Just do a Google search to find them.

Ideally you want to have a room or a spot in your living space that is dedicated to sitting in meditation. You can include in this area anything you feel supports your practice. In my zendo I have an area rug, upon which we place our zafus directly in front of a small Buddha statue and several candles. I also have a singing bowl and certain gifts from friends who have been supportive of my practice. I keep this area as sacrosanct and do not allow any activity to take place there other than sitting or quiet peaceful discussion directly after sitting.

It is important to treat your meditation space as a sacred spot, and that it be shown proper respect. This reflects your own commitment to sitting and will aid you in finding a deeper and more fulfilling meditation experience. If it's not possible to have one space reserved only for sitting, then the idea of sitting at the same time everyday becomes more important as that also becomes a sacred time which aids your meditation practice.

We begin by seating ourselves in a stable manner. Contrary to popular belief you do not have to sit in the most painful position to meditate. The second most painful will do. Just kidding. The reason we pick a posture has to do with how stable it makes us and what enhances our experience. Stability is important, as we do not want to move during our sitting period. You can choose any of the following postures and may wish to experiment with which one grants you the greatest feeling of stability.

Postures

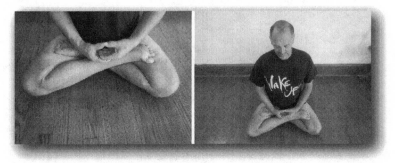

Full Lotus

First there is the full lotus position. If you are very limber and can sit in this position for ten to fifteen minutes without crying like a baby, (I personally can not), this is the most stable of the positions and is desirable for that reason and also because you can impress other Buddhists by showing that you are so spiritually evolved that you can sit in full lotus. (Just kidding about the second reason...sort of.) The mantra for this position is "Owwwwww!!!"

Half Lotus

The half lotus is similar to the full lotus in that it requires a certain amount of dexterity and is also a very stable position. In addition, although it is not as cool as the full lotus, no one is going to take your lunch money because you sit in this position either. Non-meditators will also be very impressed. What do they know?

Burmese

For those who are not interested in impressing their Buddhist friends, and whose knees do not allow for the other two lotus positions, there is the Burmese sitting position. It is similar to the full and half lotus positions except that the feet remain on the floor and the legs never actually cross each other. This is much easier on the knees and ankles though not as stable as the lotus positions. Also, you'll be considered cool in Burma.

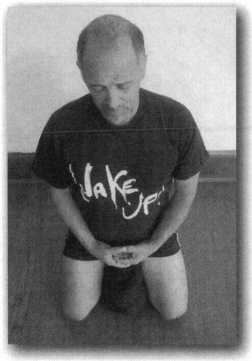

Kneeling

Place a cushion between your legs with your feet supine under your buttocks on either side of the cushion. This is also a fairly stable position and less pretzel-like than those in the lotus family. Very few cool points go to those who sit this way, but if you are already overflowing with coolness (as I'm sure you are since you are reading this book) that is not an issue.

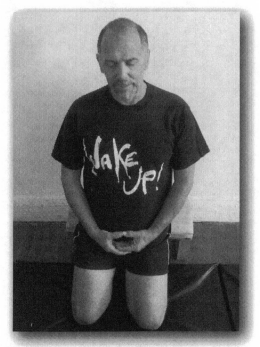

Seza Bench

The sitting position on a seza bench is similar to the kneeling position but differs in that you actually have a device that helps you maintain that position. In both this and the kneeling position I should caution you that your knees must be strong to remain in these positions for any length of time. If you have any weakness in your knees these positions would not be advisable for you to try. The seza bench may be preferable if you are just starting out and do not feel comfortable with the lotus postures yet and it also comes in handy for long sitting periods.

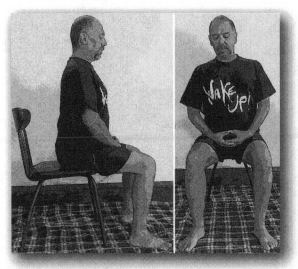

Sitting in a Straight Backed Chair

Sit on a regular chair positioned forward, so that your back is not resting against the backrest. This is the best position for those of us who have any physical concerns around our legs. (Your bus pass may be in jeopardy with this one.)

Lying Down

This has never been a posture I have enjoyed but there are many who do. The two main things to keep in mind are that if you lay in this position place at least one of your hands over your solar plexus. (This is an Edgar Cayce teaching.) Also, do not do this on your bed as you will be subject to sleep energy. If you overcome that, it may transform the sleep energy in your bed to one of wakefulness.

All of these positions are viable alternatives that lend themselves to a productive Za Zen meditation session. Besides, no one will think you are really cool until you attain enlightenment.

Posture

Whatever position you choose it is essential that you keep a straight line between the base of your spine and the top of your head. It may take a while for you to strengthen the muscles in your back to where you are strong enough to do this for longer than ten or fifteen minutes. Do not be concerned if your back hurts a little at first. You can expect that your legs will probably fall asleep. When I first started sitting I scared myself with thoughts of needing an amputation if I cut off the blood flow for too long. Then a teacher reminded me that no one has ever died from a sleeping limb. Your sitting will get stronger with practice.

Mudras

The position of the hands is especially significant in sitting Za Zen. The position of the hands is called a mudra. At this point all you really need to know is that the mudra is there to help you keep track of how well you are doing in achieving an optimal meditative state.

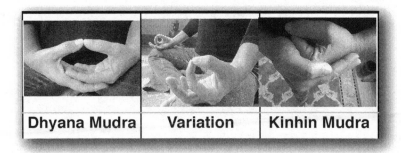

| Dhyana Mudra | Variation | Kinhin Mudra |

Place the right hand down, palm up, and the left hand down, palm up on top of the right, and connect the very tips of the thumbs just barely touching. This forms the mudra in the illustrations, called the Dhyana Mudra.

The word *Dhyana* is Sanskrit for meditation. When it reached China *Dhyana* became *Cha'an* and when it came to Japan it became *Zen*. All of these words mean meditation, therefore Zen Buddhism simply means meditation Buddhism.

One purpose of the mudra is as a barometer for you to check in while you are sitting. If you are straining or trying too hard the thumbs will come together and there will be pressure between the tips. If you are spacing out or too unfocused the thumbs will come apart and be separated. The position you want to maintain with your hands is to have the thumb tips just lightly touching each other.

A variation of the Dhyana Mudra is accomplished by placing hands separately on the knees with palms up and the thumb and index or middle fingers barley touching. Again, the thumbs can be used in the same manner as a barometer for your level of concentration in meditation.

For walking meditation, or kinhin, the left hand is formed into a fist and placed knuckles out on the abdomen while the right hand covers it with fingers extended.

Focus on the Breath

A seeker once asked the Buddha, "What is the difference between you and me?" The seeker wanted to know what it was exactly that separated the Buddha from regular people like himself who were not enlightened masters.

The Buddha replied, "The difference between you and me is that when I am breathing in, I know that I am breathing in."

This is a very profound statement. Being aware of your breath means you are fully grounded and awake in the present moment. Breathing is the most present thing we do and when we focus on it we cannot help but be grounded in the present moment. Since that is the very state we hope to achieve when sitting, we use our breath as a focal point.

With each in breath, we mentally say the word "IN," and with each out breath we mentally say the word "OUT."

Do not seek to change anything about your breathing or anything else while you are sitting. Just take the ten to fifteen minutes to try and spend as much time as you can while you focus only on your breathing. Follow each breath in and out. That's it. Sound easy? Give it a try. See how long you can go just focusing on your breath and being present.

The Train Station

One of the most persistent misunderstandings around meditation, as I mentioned above, is the idea that you need to empty your mind of all thoughts. I'm not sure where this came from but I can be reasonably sure it didn't come from anyone who actually meditated. I don't know if you have ever tried to make your mind a complete blank this way but it is a very good method for making yourself crazy, hence not a very good thing to do in meditation.

Your mind has thoughts running through it. When you first start to meditate your thoughts are usually very loud and seductive. They carry you off on long trips and before you know it you're somewhere else and not present. This is the very thing we are trying to address through meditation but we do not address anything by trying to suppress it. Suppression is the surest way to make certain that whatever it is you want to reduce will intensify in magnitude and frequency.

Think of your mind as a busy train station and the thoughts running through it as trains. It is not surprising that trains run through a train station. That's what a train station is for. Your mind is a train station for thoughts. That's what it is for as well. The idea is not to stop the trains from running but to remain in the station watching them pass by and not get on any of them.

At first your mind/station will feel like rush hour with lots of trains and lots of activity. We reduce the traffic and ease the congestion not by trying to suppress it but by letting the trains/thoughts run on. Eventually rush hour ends and the intensity of activity starts to slow down and become more manageable. This is a natural process that happens when we do not try to interfere while remaining mindful. After sitting for a while longer this activity will start to level off even more and eventually will come to resemble a station in a rural area with only a few trains scheduled every day.

The idea is to sit in the station and watch the trains go by. We aim to remain in the station and not take any trips during this period of sitting. There will be plenty of time to ride the trains after the meditation is over.

However despite our best intentions sometimes we lose focus and find ourselves several miles out of town watching the scenery and realize that we reflexively took a trip. If you do happen to find yourself on a train taking a trip, don't fight it or lose patience with yourself. Very gently return the focus to your breath, which will allow you to return to the station. Breathing in and breathing out. Remember that what you are attempting to do does not happen overnight and your habits are still ascendant.

Give yourself a break and be loving and forgiving of your missteps along the way.

Timer

I suggest when you first begin not to try and do too much. Five, ten or fifteen minutes is fine for beginning a practice. In fact anytime you can take at least one conscious breath is productive. As the Buddha said, knowing you are breathing in while you are breathing in is a very powerful means of bringing yourself into the present moment, and that is what we are hoping to accomplish more and more as we practice meditation. In fact, the ability to take at least one conscious breath can be used as a sort of mini portable form of meditation. It is a good skill to acquire as you can use it anywhere and at any time. It is especially handy in times of stress.

Begin with the amount of time that feels right for you and will allow you to sit consistently. Don't push yourself to do more than you feel comfortable doing. You can gradually increase your periods of sitting until you find the proper time for your needs. It is better to sit too briefly than to sit too long. You can have a bad experience by sitting too long and it could make returning to sit more difficult. You want to make it as positive an experience as you can while you are working to build a habit of sitting.

There are several ways to time yourself that will not overly intrude into your meditation. I have in the past set up my wristwatch in a position where my eyes do not have to move too much to find it. A better alternative and one that I use is an app which is available for iPhone and Android called the Insight Meditation Timer (available at https://insighttimer.com) which allows you to set a time and chimes or wood block sounds that actually enhance your experience of meditation and free you from the need to watch a clock. It also has a journaling feature that is very nice. It is free, and there are guided meditations available (some paid) that can be very helpful to beginning and advanced meditators and a thriving online community.

Discipline

Try to develop a discipline around sitting. I have been sitting regularly for over twenty years and I still have to struggle sometimes to get myself to sit. Inertia and momentum play a big part in this ability to sit regularly. The more you do it and the more consistently you do it, the easier it is to continue and develop a deep practice. If you take time off or miss a few days it gets progressively harder to sit again. Then it takes getting really uncomfortable as you get farther and farther out of tune and sense a critical mass build-up of tension before you feel you have no choice but to sit. Then you do sit and all of the tension releases and you scratch your head afterwards wondering why the heck you didn't just sit in the first place? Trust me, we all go through it. Experienced meditators have all gone through this more than once. Don't let it stop you.

If things come up and you miss a day, do not get down on yourself. This is a difficult thing to do and you will face a lot of resistance from your ego. Simply forgive yourself and sit when you can do so. Discipline is very important so try to strike a balance. You may have to push yourself to sit at times but find a good middle ground where you are not beating yourself up, but also not letting yourself slack off. As you continue to practice, the discipline will come to you more easily as your mind becomes less noisy.

Part of the discipline you must develop is the ability to resist urges to fix things while you are sitting. Once you have begun a period of meditation you should not move unless there is an emergency. If your house is on fire or the baby is screaming or something of that nature occurs, please interrupt your sit and take care of what you need to do. But if the phone rings or you get an itch or a nagging pain or your leg falls asleep, do not move to fix these things. Allow them to be what they are and allow yourself to learn the lesson they are teaching you. See them as opportunities for learning about arising and ceasing and watch your reflexes try to take over. Do it consistently enough and you will begin to free yourself of habitual behaviors. The implications of this skill are tremendous.

Introducing Mara

When the Buddha was about to attain enlightenment, it was Mara, the god whose job it is to tempt us from away from our spiritual life, who sought to distract Siddhartha from his purpose. The Buddha did not allow himself to be moved by anything Mara tried and so he achieved enlightenment.

One of the things you can count on as you develop a sitting practice is that you are going to become well acquainted with Mara and his tactics. While trying to sit, you will itch in places you didn't know could itch. The more you break and scratch, the more the itching will multiply. You will experience pains and aches and uncomfortable and scary thoughts.

Early on in my sitting I used to think about letting go. I knew that's what I was supposed to do but every time I sat I could still feel the tension in my body. Mara seized upon this concern and I started worrying that though I would try to let go it never worked. This left me more frustrated and farther from my goal of letting go. Mara was doing his job. In response to this I tried letting go of letting go. Not being any more successful I realized after a long time that the letting go is something that happens naturally and organically over time and with a consistent practice. Paradoxically we let go by embracing that which we are trying to overcome. I rose above Mara and sitting got a lot easier.

Mara will even get to you before you sit by whispering in your head about how well you have been doing and that you don't even really need to sit anymore. Or remind you of things you'd rather be doing than sitting. Mara does not want you to sit. So who the heck is Mara and what's his deal?

Mara is nothing more than a symbol for our own egos. The illusive selves that we identify with, the names and qualities and physical traits and character flaws and memories and everything else that goes into building the illusion that what we are is not a spiritual being but somehow a separate individual who has somehow created itself.

The ego is represented as a major demon here to symbolize what the ego becomes when we forget that it is a creation made of illusions. It is there to help us function in this world, but in the end it's just a tool and nothing more. The problem is that we have enthroned the tool and identified with it. The ego believes it is what you are, and any effort to dethrone it is an act of self-destruction. So, it fights back.

I must have an identity in order to communicate and function within the context of the world. A separate "self" is very useful for that purpose. I call myself "Marshall" and I respond to that name or sound. I join in a social contract with everyone else that this sound will symbolize "me." If not for this how would we ever know whom we were addressing? I suppose we could go through a list of characteristics like "Hey you, man with the graying hair and the red shirt and the jeans that have a slight hole in the knee," ...but you can see how soon that would get old. For the sake of brevity, we all agree to treat this fiction of a name and identity as though it were factual.

The problem occurs when I start to really identify with this sound and mistake it for an actual "self," which does not in fact exist as a separate entity.

This apparent conflict of what we believe and what is real causes our perception to distort and tells the ego to work to cover all traces of spiritual knowledge that might lead to its unmasking as an impostor, along with its concurrent relegation back to the tool box where it belongs. In response, the ego grows and works to blind us, becoming puffed up with pride and longings and fears and avoidances and grasping, transforming itself from a useful idea that enhances communication to a monstrous tyrant that strictly regulates what information comes in and what goes out.

The ego believes it is you and that your very existence is dependent on this activity, and so the closer you get to Truth the more energetic its exertions will become to distract you. But the ego is not evil - its intentions are good. It believes it is saving us from annihilation.

Therefore, when you begin to sit and as your practice intensifies and begins to bear fruit, expect greater resistance from your ego in concurrently stronger and more ingenious ways. With the Buddha, Mara had to go all out with demon armies and luscious daughters etc., but when you begin to practice Mara need only put your leg to sleep or cause an itch or a pain and voila - you are distracted. This is Mara's whole purpose.

When this occurs, do not resist the ego's exertions by pushing back. That feeds the beast and makes the manifestations stronger. Do not allow yourself to be motivated by fear. Fear is the tool of the ego. Allow fears to be and trust that they are not real or relevant. Understand that through the ignorance of the ego, it believes it is saving your life and its intentions are wholly for your good as it sees it. It is just totally ignorant of the True nature of the universe, and so acts in a manner that sabotages our attempts to grow spiritually.

Given its isolation from Truth, it is no wonder the ego/Mara is mistaken as to what you really need. Treat it as an old friend who gives bad advice. Think of it as a drunken uncle who corners you during a family get together and tells you how you should be living your life. You won't hate him and you won't fear him, but you won't take his advice too seriously either. Smile and appreciate the misguided attempts, the signs of care and concern, but see the advice for what it is. When you experience itches, know that this is the ego trying to distract you in order to save you. Thank it and continue to experience the itch without seeking to change it.

At every boundary you cross there will be a barrier set up by your ego. Built into that boundary will be an alarm system made of fear, and set there to warn you back and keep you from crossing. The farther you develop, the more intense will be the resistance. Simply know that whatever it is you encounter has no power to stop you. Understand that perhaps once this was necessary but it no longer is. Thank it for guarding and protecting you and let it go by as you expand beyond the comfort zone of that particular boundary. Once you cross that boundary, you'll find there isn't the terrible picture that ego has painted, but instead another step taken toward freedom.

In the end, when you are free, Mara is not destroyed but instead becomes your servant as was always intended. Just like the Buddha on his awakening, you have to put Mara in his proper place. He was no longer called Siddhartha after his enlightenment - he is called the Buddha. Siddhartha was the name of his ego and individual personality. He still had access to all of his memories and experiences as Siddhartha when he became the Buddha; he just wasn't bound by it anymore. Remember you are the master and Mara is your servant.

Attributes Gained in Practice

Meditation, in Buddhism, is referred to as "practice." There is a very practical aspect to it, and very real and practical resulting abilities that come along with a strong practice along the path to enlightenment.

The growth you experience will be gradual and can be so subtle that there may come a time when one day after sitting for a while you realize you are not the same person you were when you began your practice of sitting. I mean, you are the same person of course, but actually you feel even more "you" than you did before. You feel freer because you are.

It's similar to the way an hour hand moves on an old analog clock. It is too slow and gradual to see the movement but we know it has moved because with the passage of time it is somewhere else. In the same way, as you practice over the passage of time, you will become a much better version of yourself.

Remember, this is all about freedom from suffering. As you continue to sit, you will experience that freedom in more and more profound ways. But this is not the only benefit of sitting. There are mental, physical and spiritual benefits as well.

Mental, Physical and Spiritual Health

Disciplining and calming the mind has an impact that is most notable in the mind itself. Thoughts become more organized and easier to sort through. It's as though each session of sitting carries out some of the rubbish that has cluttered your mind and organizes the rest of it into the proper filing cabinets. Thought becomes faster and easier as there is less dependence on *trying* to think. More ease is developed in allowing intuition and instinct to work hand in hand with cognition. The strain is taken out of cognition and replaced with the experience of a peaceful and efficient mind.

The calmer mind finds it easier to make judgments, since the untrue and illusive thoughts are seen for what they are and discarded as irrelevant. Confusion becomes a rare occurrence and creative thinking becomes a more and more common experience. Mistrust of your own mind is replaced with confidence as your thinking bears more and more fruit and is validated by actual experience. Emotions that used to cloud your thinking become less intense and disruptive, and begin to work in concert with your mind to improve your daily functioning in the world to give you a fuller, more multi-dimensional view of what is before you.

Calming the emotions, and the concurrent sense of peace that engenders, also has an impact on the body. Remember our discussion before of how the body is like a guitar? Eastern medicine defines energy centers with the body called chakras. These chakras all vibrate at a different frequency just like a stringed instrument. As with a guitar, if the strings are left out of tune for a long period of time this can actually warp the neck and create problems in the body of the guitar. In your body, the chakras are like your strings. Leaving them out of tune causes stress that has an injurious effect on the body. Through meditation we retune the chakras to vibrate at their optimum frequency. When they are all in tune, you experience harmony. It's really that simple.

Stress becomes eased and even when experienced, transforms back to peaceful states more quickly since the processes are allowed to complete themselves without interference. Stress has a very injurious impact on the body and chronic stress is a killer. One of the greatest effects of a regular practice is the melting away of all forms of stress. Conditions related to stress such as headaches, heart problems, rashes etc. become less intense and more rare experiences. Physical well-being becomes the rule rather than the exception.

Calming the mind and the body allows for a deep exploration of the spiritual, which is not possible when one is worried or confused or in pain. The concurrent peace allows one to see beauty in all things and encounter a profound sense of being a part of a wonderful and loving universe. No words or teacher could ever convey this feeling to you, but a regular practice of sitting will bring you to it on a daily basis. Seeing deeply as a result of the intimacy you develop with stillness and silence, allows you to tune in to the voice of wisdom that is always present in everything.

To understand why stillness and silence are so important, let me draw you a thought picture. I referred to this earlier in the book but here I shall expand and illustrate it more fully.

Imagine all of your chakras, which relate to different levels of consciousness, are like radios lined up. To the left the radio at the end is playing acid rock and is turned up to maximum volume. The next one moving right is playing classic rock and is turned up to nine. The next is playing soft rock and is turned up to 7. On down the line the radios become quieter and more peaceful. With the loudest radio turned up all the way, even though the other radios are playing, they cannot be heard. In meditation what we are doing has the effect of lowering the volume on those outer radios so that in the end you can clearly hear the quietest and softest radio on the right. It is tuned to WBNR, Buddha Nature Radio, bringing you all the hits and sounds of the Buddha 24/7. In the Judeo/Christian tradition this soft voice is called the still small voice of G-d. The wisdom here is always available to you. It is always waiting for you to get quiet enough to be able to hear it. Isn't the ultimate goal of all Spirituality to be able to experience Universal Truth?

In this quiet and peaceful place you reconnect with the Source of all things. The book of the ages is opened to you. You become one with the universe and everything in it. Paradoxically, by releasing the striving to control everything and developing a sense of trust in the beneficence of the universe and the source of all things, you feel more in control than you ever have before.

Balance

Each time you sit you re-attune yourself to be at optimal frequency, which means you are operating in harmony with everything else and living in balance. You develop a state of equanimity that becomes more and more solid and stable the longer you practice. You reach a point where things that would have thrown you into states of imbalance in the past now find you like a tree that can bend with the wind without being uprooted.

As you live in the present moment more and more frequently and become used to it, you will experience the one-dimensionality and illusory nature of the concepts of past and future, freeing you from past guilt and future worry. Guilt is always a creature of the past, just as worry is a creature of the future. When the illusion of these concepts is plain to you, guilt and worry have no hold on you and dissipate like a shadow in the sun.

Presence

Through a strong practice you find yourself being more and more aware and sensitive to what is happening in every moment. You become more empathic and compassionate to those around you. You begin to see deeply into those things which seek to disturb your peace and find ways to let fears dissipate. You develop a greater trust of all of your senses, including the more ethereal ones like intuition and dreams.

The symbols that you confront everyday in your life begin to share their meanings with you. Your understanding and depth of knowledge and wisdom become truly profound. The confidence this engenders in you causes those around you to trust you, instinctively understanding that there is something about you they can rely on. As you become more effective in helping others, it feeds the cycle of compassion and desire to help within you as well. This is a desire that is very strong in liberated people.

Sight

I hesitate to mention this at all since there is so much misunderstanding about it, but the fact is that as your practice deepens, you will also begin to develop rudimentary parapsychological abilities. Your intuition and instincts become clearer and more available to you.

A "psychic" is someone who is able to tune in to the quieter radios. We are all potential psychics.

It is not supernatural but supremely natural that you can see deeply into the heart of reality and know things that do not come from the finite mind or simple cognition.

I used to teach classes in Psychic phenomena and related subjects, having attended grad school for it. I'm horrified by the number of people who are ready to exploit and take advantage of those who are naturally curious and are looking for answers to very important questions. They build themselves up to be modern day oracles that can perform miracles, which no ordinary person believes they could ever hope to achieve. The simple truth of the matter is that we all have psychic abilities and can learn to become our own oracles without being taken to the cleaners or surrendering our own best judgment to someone we believe has a special gift not available to us.

As you begin to free your mind, it is only logical that these abilities would become more manifest. The ability to hear what is very quiet becomes easier for you. You naturally become aware of gifts that were always available to you and only awaited you getting quiet enough to claim them.

That being said, it's very important to remember that these effects are not a goal in themselves nor are they even a sign of spiritual evolution. These intuitive and seemingly supernatural knowing experiences are just a sign that you are getting in touch with the more subtle and quieter things in your consciousness. They have nothing to do with freedom from suffering. If you allow them to become yet another thing to grasp for and they can, indeed, become the cause of more suffering. They are a tool to help you on your journey toward liberation and nothing more.

The Buddha avoided this topic altogether because he felt it would distract from the important work of freeing us. I wholeheartedly agree and only mention it here as a caution. Mara will use this and other "spiritual" experiences to distract from your real goal. Do not become enchanted by this shiny item. It is a byproduct and a tool to help you, nothing more. Remember, everyone has these abilities so there is nothing special about anyone who develops them.

Persistence

In order to succeed at anything, you have to experience failure many, many times. The one difference between those who succeed and those who do not is that the successful allow nothing to stop them from pursuing their goal. Failure is only what you experience when you stop short of your goal. Failure is a way station and a lesson, not the end.

You will have days when you do not want to sit or things just come up or a million other reasons supplied by your own personal Mara. Sometimes you win the battle and sometimes you lose. Accept that from the outset and you cannot fail. You only fail when you allow failure to become a permanent reality rather than a temporary setback.

I have been meditating for over thirty years, and some days I still struggle to get myself to sit. Some days I win and some days I lose. Some days I am too ill to sit or something else unavoidably keeps me from my cushion. I breathe and accept this and do what I can. Keep going. You will succeed.

In the *Jataka Tales,* the Buddha puts off full enlightenment for over five hundred lifetimes so that he could develop the ten perfections and become a full Teaching Buddha. He persisted through all of those lives and all of the setbacks and with patient persistence found his way through. If you are reading this you have lived through much to get you here as well. Keep going!

But I recognize there are times when doing a full sit is just not an option. For those times I would like to suggest mini meditations that are more effective the stronger your regular sitting practice becomes.

The first is conscious breathing that involves nothing more than being aware of each in breath and each out breath just as we do when we are training ourselves to sit. In this case though we can do this anywhere. You can be driving a car, feel tension rise in you and take one or two conscious breaths. This will help center you and place you back in the here and now.

There is also a Loving Kindness meditation you can do in addition to conscious breathing. This can also be done at the end of a meditation session. It is a very simple and very powerful method for changing your heart and mind and granting you peace and happiness. Begin by saying, "I am happy, I am healthy, I am safe, I am at peace." Once you feel that you can accomplish this and really feel the Truth of it, you can then move on to the next step. Don't rush it. It may take a while but eventually you will feel the joy and peace rise in you.

The next step in Loving Kindness meditation (also known as Metta) is to apply the same words, but rather than to yourself, to people you feel close to and love. You may even find this easier than doing it for yourself.

The next step is to repeat the process for those you would consider acquaintances for whom you have no strong feelings one way or another but for whom you would like to see experience happiness, health, safety and peace.

Finally you get to the graduate level of Metta. This entails repeating this process for those you find yourself in conflict with. It may take a while. At first you may find yourself repeating the words in your head while clenching your teeth. That is okay - just keep practicing. After a while you will feel the animosity lessen and feel your heart grow lighter. This is a wonderful practice that you can do anytime including and especially in moments when someone has rubbed you the wrong way.

Forgiveness is not only good for the object of your ire but for you as well. The Buddha once said that holding on to anger is like holding a hot coal in your hand. You may be able to throw it at your enemy and may even injure them but you will certainly feel the pain of your burned hand either way.

Remember, the voice of Truth, Wisdom, and Universal Knowledge is always available to you if you are willing to learn to get quiet enough to hear it. All of the answers you have been looking for in every corner of the world and in every other person in the world are actually right there within your own Buddha Nature, patiently waiting for you to become quiet and still enough so that it can instruct you.

It was through meditation that the Buddha became enlightened. During this process, one of the experiences he had was the re-emergence of memories of countless past lives.

CHAPTER SIX

Birth, Death, Rebirth

The Wave

Once there was a great ocean whose surface was very calm, like a perfect mirror of the sky. Before long a small wind began blowing across the surface of the ocean and it created ripples. The wind continued to increase in intensity and before long the ripples became waves.

One such wave born that day became aware of itself. Its first thought was, "What am I?" As he continued his journey across the ocean he looked for clues and signs that would give him the answer. He knew that many things joined with him for a time on his journey; plankton, seaweed, fish, sharks, whales and even plastic bottles that formed a great island of trash. But he noticed that though these objects travelled with him for a while, inevitably all of it passed through him and was left behind. The wave was not these objects he encountered even though they did seem to actually join with him for a time.

As his journey continued and the wind continued to blow he felt himself getting taller and bigger. He discovered the bottom of the ocean one day when his foot touched something solid below it. He saw that he and his brother waves were heading straight for what appeared to be an island far in the distance, and one by one he witnessed the waves before him crash on the beach and become no more. He knew that this would be his fate as well.

"If only I could get an answer to this question of what I am, it would be alright," he thought. Finally he approached the beach, crested and crashed upon the shore. Just as he was falling back through the sand towards the water he understood.

"Ah, I am the ocean."

Fear of Death

The Buddha said that every sentient being fears death. It is the one great fear that ties all sentient beings together and is at the core of so much suffering.

Once, when my son was very young, he was in the hospital to have tubes placed in his ears to prevent the ear infections to which he was prone. I went downstairs for coffee and happened to find myself in the same corridor as the emergency room.

A security guard stepped out of the E.R. and looked at me with a horrified expression. "What are you doing here?" he asked. "Never mind," he added. "Just stand back and avert your eyes."

Of course this aroused my curiosity so I had to look. Shortly thereafter a gurney was wheeled out of the E.R. that had a body on it covered by a sheet. "That was it?" I thought. Seeing a dead body is apparently such a taboo in our culture that great lengths are taken to ensure nobody sees one. I felt like Siddhartha being sheltered by his father from the horrible truth that death comes to everyone.

Apparently, hospital security works to clear the corridors so that no one has to confront this awful truth. They actually clear the halls so that they can transport the dead in secret ensuring nobody has to face the reality and the inevitability of mortality. That was why the guard was so horrified when he saw me there.

I found the experience very instructive as to how we deal with death as a society. I think it is why we have nursing homes where we shut away our parents and grandparents. It wasn't that long ago those elderly family members lived with their families until they passed. Now we shut them away as if we can deny the fact of death and dying.

I should say in the interest of full disclosure that my mother is currently in a facility. We cared for her at home for 6 years but her needs progressed beyond our ability to address them sufficiently. So now she lives in a facility in Pittsburgh and my sister visits her several times a week. I fly up when I am home and see her as well. There are times when a facility is a good alternative but not to be used as a dumping ground in which to place your parents and then ignore them.

Death is an important part of life and holds essential lessons for us. All things that arise eventually cease. If we deny endings we avoid finishing. We go against the nature of things and create more suffering.

Much of what the Buddha taught involved the conquering of death. Although he was loath to discuss supernatural or metaphysical phenomenon, he did weave it into much of what he taught. It was impossible to address the suffering of sentient beings without doing so. You have to remember that the Buddha and all of his disciples were surrounded by the Hindu religion. In fact before there was a Buddha, just about everyone was Hindu in that part of the world. Reincarnation, the gods and different realms of existence are all a big part of the Hindu beliefs.

There was nothing revolutionary in the Buddha discussing fortunate rebirth or reincarnation or different realms of existence. It was taken for granted in the India of 2600 years ago. The belief was so ubiquitous that it would be like taking time to identify that we are surrounded by air, a condition that no one ever questions.

The one difference the Buddha had with Hinduism, and this was a big one, was the denial of the existence of an Atman, or separate self, that reincarnates. Remember the Buddha taught that there is no permanent separate self.

But he did not reject reincarnation; he just came at it from a different angle.

But to mix the belief and faith in reincarnation as a Buddhist thing would be a big mistake. One does not have to believe in reincarnation in order to practice Buddhism whose real focus is on the cessation of suffering. It is only in the relevance of rebirth as a source for the continuity of suffering that it plays a part at all. One does not have to go beyond or before this life to address their suffering.

Remember that everything is a process. It is in allowing these processes to complete that we are liberated from the suffering. In order to allow these processes to complete we must embrace the importance of the nature of cessation.

You cannot embrace the natural place of cessation in all processes and exclude death. It's all or nothing. This is why so much of what the Buddha taught had something to do with death.

Tibetan Buddhists are especially interested in the role of a good death in order to find enlightenment.

Remember the law of impermanence applies to us as well as everything else. This is not a pleasant thought when you are convinced that who and what you are is tied to this body that you know is finite.

I remember as a small child lying awake in my bed one night after my Grandmother died, trying to imagine the oblivion that I believed one day would become my fate. I had to concentrate to make myself focus on the fact that death was not a supposition, but an inevitable occurrence that one day sooner or later, I would meet. When I was able to fully believe it and visualize it, the thought was overwhelmingly terrifying and erased any possibility at all of security or safety.

Now as I have gotten older this issue becomes a bigger and more immediate concern. I very recently underwent a heart transplant, so I'm intimately aware of my own mortality. What the Buddha has to say about this is especially important if you or a loved one are facing a life threatening illness. Of course to be totally honest, being born is a life threatening illness. It is actually a great gift to be able to face one's mortality. Facing mortality is difficult, but also full of lessons about how to live one's life.

We tend to deny the fact of our own mortality and think we have a guarantee if nothing immediate threatens us. I remember many years ago when I was in the hospital after my first heart attack and a group of men including my father were all looking at me with pity on their faces. I had to laugh because it hit me at that moment how deluded they were, thinking that just because I was in the hospital bed they would outlive me. As of this date none of those men are still on Earth. It is important to remember that we can pass on at anytime, but this should not be a cause for fear.

I believe all of us live under this cloud (the awareness of mortality) to a greater or lesser degree. I further believe that this one underlying fear is at the heart of 99% of our suffering and that only by coming to terms and finding peace with it can we begin to emerge into a lighter and freer way of life. Fear is behind all suffering. If you look at all clinging and all avoidance, you are looking at the seeds of fear. You can see that what they have in common is a denial of the law of impermanence and a putting off of the inevitable lesson we must learn.

Fear is the absence or opposite of Buddha Nature. It is an intense feeling that something is wrong, which of course is correct so long as we are not being true to who and what we really are. And since death or loss is the greatest fear of all, liberation demands that we come to terms with it so that we can be liberated. This is what the Buddha meant when he used the word liberation. But there is good news.

The good news is that once you come to terms with death and face it, like all nightmares when confronted, it turns out to be not nearly the monster you thought it was.

The Other Fear of Death

Of course the other and perhaps more difficult fear we live with is that of losing someone who is close to us. This is, in some ways, much harder on the one left behind than it is on the one who goes. It's also inevitable, though who will be the one to go and who will be the survivor in any given relationship will vary. No matter how strong the bond or how many protestations of "I

Will Never Leave You," made as sincerely as possible, all relationships end in separation of one sort or another. It is the nature of the beast.

Those who know and understand this have a choice. They can live in constant fear and anxiety over losing lovers, relations, friends, pets, co-workers, etc. and get by through a daily exercise of heavy denial. Or they can learn to accept the reality of the situation and spend every moment with those they love in full appreciation of what they have.

When we lose someone we will naturally feel grief and sadness. This sadness will turn into out and out suffering if we have not made peace with the realities of the impermanence of relationships, and accepted it as a part of life. We should not waste all the time we have together being afraid of the eventual separation, but instead enjoy and appreciate each precious moment we get to spend together.

All grief is temporary. The depth and longevity of that suffering is determined by how willing we are to accept what is, and by how well we were able to be present with our beloved while they are still present with us.

Ultimately we will all meet again anyway, so even the separations are impermanent. But the road we travel to get to that place can either be long and tortuous or short and beautiful. The choice is entirely up to us.

Fearing Change as Death

In a tarot deck there is a major arcana card called Death, which is usually symbolized by some sort of death imagery. The card is not a harbinger of actual physical death, however, but a symbol of change. Death is an archetypal image for change, which is very telling since those of us who crave security feed ourselves the illusion that we can protect ourselves from changes we do not want.

Many of us want to feel some sense of security and so we buy insurance and alarm systems and locks and stocks and IRAs and all sorts of things that we feel will give us some security. Alan Watts wrote a great book entitled "The Wisdom Of Insecurity," which argues that the search for security is a huge illusion of permanence in this world in which nothing is permanent. It is the cause of a lot of pain and suffering. This is very close to what the Buddha had to say on the subject.

If you just look deeply at what actually manifests in this world and the processes all things go through, you will see there is nothing that does not undergo constant change.

The End of Fear

According to the Buddha all beings fear death. This certainly does appear to be true. It is the last great mystery and one that cannot be pierced until we go through it. By that point it is too late to learn not to be afraid, since it's already past. So we spend our lives fearing the end of life and that keeps us from truly living our lives.

All beings have this in common. All animals will move away from that which threatens their lives. It is for this reason that the Buddha and many Buddhists are vegetarians. In fact the Buddha made the rainy season a time of retreat so as to keep the Monks from having to walk the muddy roads and inevitably stepping on and killing worms. The Bikkhus who followed the Buddha had few possessions but one which everyone was required to have was a water strainer so as to filter out the microorganisms and small creatures when drinking water so that none would be harmed. I myself am a pescatarian, meaning I eat seafood but no meat. You must do what feels right to you.

Fear is a Universal Experience

All beings suffer from fear, but not all fear is bad or unnatural.

There is a difference between situational and adaptive fear - such as one develops about putting ones hand in a fire - and neurotic fear. Certainly it is a good thing to feel anxiety about getting too close to a flame. This is adaptive to a very real situation that could result in injury and even death if not heeded. I would call this situational or appropriate fear. It appears in response to an actual situation and lasts only as long as the perceived threat is apparent. Once the danger has passed, the emotion fades as well. I want to stress that there is nothing wrong with this type of fear and anyone can see the value of it.

Then there is neurotic fear, which is a fear that manifests as a result of unskillful thinking and is not linked to any actual present danger. This type of fear is chronic and hangs on stubbornly to its manifestation.

Whereas it is adaptive and helpful to have the information that sticking one's hand in a fire can hurt and to feel a sensation of fear which would tend to keep you from doing that, a general fear of fire is non-adaptive and could actually cause a different type of harm to you. Suppose you found yourself out in the woods and needed a fire to keep warm but were too afraid of fire to light one. That is the type of fear that cripples us, making us lose sight of the magnificent and all-powerful creatures we are.

These neurotic fears that we collect and carry around are the very things that in the guise of keeping us safe instead keep us bound as prisoners.

But of all the neurotic fears we can have, one is fairly universal and is the cause of the greatest amount of suffering. That is the fear of death. In order to free ourselves from suffering we must free ourselves from all neurotic fears, and at the root of all neurotic fear is this archetypal fear of death.

Overcoming this fear is the key to regaining equanimity and peace. Your most precious possession is your equanimity and peace. It is your birthright and at the very core of your nature. Nothing can ever make you lose it. No matter how far you drift from that state, it is the default position to which you will return whenever you allow yourself to be present and just be. This central part of our True Nature we call Love. Love is at the essence of all there is.

Love is the fabric of everything that exists. We are composed of nothing but love. Fear is the sensation we feel when we experience the absence of love. It is not actually possible to be anywhere where there is not love manifesting, but we are certainly capable of making ourselves believe in things that are not so. We build whole worlds of illusion based on fear and lose sight of the love that is our home. We lose sight of who and what we really are. In doing so we tell ourselves scary stories of who we might be. These are the illusions we live with. We imbue them with the power of our belief. When we stop telling ourselves these scary stories and begin to just pay attention to what actually is, our sanity and true nature exert themselves. We begin to see the Truth. It is a light that dispels all the shadows we have created.

Love is the True nature of all things. It is present everywhere and in all things. It is the stuff of which the entire universe is built. That is why when we act in accordance with love and compassion, we feel wonderful. We are expressing our own True nature. When we choose otherwise, we feel the tension of going against who and what we really are.

No Fear

For the Buddhist, death is a skill one must acquire to ensure it is done well. Death is not seen as the end of life or the entrance to eternal oblivion but as with all things, simply a turning of the wheel. Remember the Yin Yang Symbol? Birth, Death, and Rebirth are just manifestations of the ever turning wheel.

What Dream?

Normally we think of birth and death in terms of birth being analogous to waking up and dying as going to sleep. In the Buddhist view that is upside down. The Buddha means the Awakened One, which begs the question, awakened from what?

In Buddhism birth is metaphorically like going to sleep. Our consciousness narrows greatly from the before birth state. The life we live in between is like dreaming that seems very real while we are in it. Death is waking up from this dream and meditation is training us to be lucid within the dream. The Buddha was able to be awake within the dream. That is what makes one enlightened.

Looking at it in this light we can see that there is nothing to fear in death. Nobody likes to wake up in the morning. Very few people wake up, jump out of bed and start whistling a happy tune. For me at least, waking up in the morning makes me thank G-d that we have the technology of snooze alarms. Suppose you're having a great dream where you are lying on a sun drenched tropical beach with a daiquiri while slave girls feed you grapes...too far? Then you wake up and it's "oh no, let me stay asleep I was just having the greatest dream". This is how we deal with the end of life. No matter the suffering involved we love our lives. We feel like we are having a great dream so we do not look forward to waking up and watching the dream dissipate into thin air. But to extend the metaphor a bit more, yes, perhaps the first moments of waking up are hard, but after a short time we may smell coffee from downstairs, the sun shining outside and the birds singing. There is nothing terrible in waking up just as there is nothing terrible in dying.

Dualism

As with the other pairs of opposites we discussed in terms of the Yin Yang symbolism of the dual nature of reality, birth and death are not two separate things that exist independently of each other. They are but two halves of the same phenomenon.

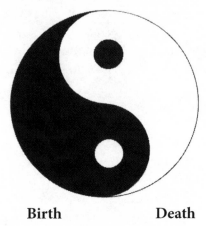

Birth   **Death**

The idea that all of reality is separated into distinct and opposing poles of manifestations is called Dualism. Dualism postulates that the world is in a constant struggle between equal and opposing forces. It is the basis of much of our literature and mythology. The idea of good winning out over evil or evil winning a final victory over good is a constant theme in most popular entertainment forms. Therefore what keeps the world and everything in it from chaos is the constant tension between the poles.

In this view that is quite prevalent in the West, we are the masters of our own fate and either we are warriors for the good or soldiers for the bad. We choose light over dark, good over bad, right over wrong, and of course we fight with every fiber of our being for life over death.

This rationale, ironically, has been at the center of many evil acts. "We're saving lives" is used as a justification for all sorts of insanity. All it takes is a moment of rational thought and an understanding of the nature of reality to see the absurdity of that statement. There is no such thing as saving lives. You can postpone death or lengthen lives but you can never save a life. Everything that is born dies, sooner or later. In fact by lengthening a life, you can concurrently be increasing the amount of suffering in that person's experience.

As the caretaker of an elderly mother with Alzheimer's, I lived with an example of how that can be every day. How many families have gone broke keeping a loved one on a respirator simply because they have the technology to do so? I am not advocating hurrying death along but I am talking about honoring the place it has in our lives. Death is not necessarily a negative phenomenon, nor is birth a totally positive one.

To the Buddhist, when it is time to die you prepare yourself and skillfully move through the process. You deal with death much as you would deal with any other process your experience has put before you, with equanimity and mindfulness.

The Buddhist view of death, as I have said, is not a cessation of existence but a transformation to another form.

Bardos

As I mentioned earlier, Tibetan Buddhism has a long tradition and much literature on the nature of the cycles of existence, which they say are divided into states called Bardos.

The time between birth and death is not seen as life but simply one bardo or phase of existence. This is followed by the bardo of dissolution or what happens during our death experience. Depending on how you do with this experience, you dwell in the next bardo of luminosity in anywhere from a profound peaceful and fully awareness realm to a fearfully delusional realm. The next bardo is of becoming, or transmigration, which leads back to the bardo of birth and life.

Cycles

The idea of a cycle of rebirth would seem to be an odd idea if it did not occur anywhere else in the natural world. The fact is that cycles are ubiquitous in nature. Take, for example, a day. The sun comes up in the morning. We call this the birth of a new day. The sun grows higher in the sky until it reaches its zenith and then it begins to descend losing power and strength as it wanes. This is like the lifetime of a single day from birth to death. The sun sets and finally there is twilight. This is like the bardo of dissolution. Then there is the nighttime where we sleep and dream. This is dwelling in the other realms. Finally the sky begins to brighten and we prepare to awaken as a new day is born.

The seasons are yet another example of the cycles within nature. In spring all new life is born; from seedlings to eggs to live births. Over the summer all life grows and thrives on to the end of summer, where it begins to slow down. In the fall the trees begin to lose their leaves and all beings prepare for winter either by denning or migrating. Finally there is winter that is the time in between where everything sleeps. And what comes after winter? Spring again, rebirth to begin another turn around the wheel.

Why should the life cycle be the exception? So this brings us up against the idea of reincarnation. Reincarnation literally means taking on a new body.

Reincarnation

In Buddhism, birth and death are like the yin yang wheel, a constantly recurring cycle. Reincarnation, or the return to new bodies and new lives, is not originally a Buddhist idea. It was such an accepted teaching in the time of the Buddha and his followers that it became a de facto part of the Buddhist thought system. Just as the concept of breathing air is not usually discussed or noted, not because it does not exist or has no effect on us, but because it is such a given that there is considered to be no need to expound on it further other than to refer to it as if everyone already knows what you mean.

Reincarnation is not an easy concept for westerners though, as it is fairly novel to our cultural mythos. This is a fairly new and exotic idea for most of us, so we need to look a little more deeply at it to understand how it works and how it fits in with Buddhist thought.

Let me say at the outset that I am not trying to convince anyone that reincarnation is real. Honestly I have been studying it for many years and in all honesty I cannot say that I know this for a fact. It is not essential for one to believe in Reincarnation in order to get the most out of Buddhist thought. Though it is important to have a good base of knowledge about what it means and how it functions within that system.

The Buddha on Reincarnation

The Buddha had distinct views on the idea of reincarnation. His main concern in teaching always centered on the Dharma and the liberation from suffering. When he discussed the cycle of rebirth (what he called the "cycle of suffering"), it was in the context of liberation from the continued return to the body. From the point of view of someone who accepts reincarnation as a fact, which he certainly did, suffering and the continued cycle of rebirth are one and the same. He taught that the ignorance, which leads to suffering also, forms the basis of continued rebirth into other forms. So when you are liberated from suffering, you are also liberated from the need to reincarnate.

The collection of 527 stories called the Jataka Tales attributed to the Buddha illustrate the use of Reincarnation as a teaching tool. In these allegories the Buddha uses stories of his past lives between the time he took the boddhisattva vows with a previous Buddha and the time he became the Buddha himself.

The Jataka Tales are not necessarily believed to come from the time of the Buddha but they are used to teach certain moral and ethical lessons, with the aim of highlighting one point or another in understanding the Dharma.

The Buddha is not portrayed as being interested in teaching about reincarnation in these stories, but told them in the context of something that was happening in the present. Often what sparked these stories were monks or lay disciples displaying odd or unusual behaviors and the Buddha making an offhand comment about where that behavior manifested before. The monks would then ask him to tell them of when this was and he would launch into a story about a past life in which he knew the target of the story and experienced the behavior in a previous life.

At the end of each story, the Buddha would identify who was who in the previous life. The Jataka stories which the Buddha relates include the experience of transmigration, which is a hundred dollar word for being reborn as forms of life other than human.

In the course of telling these stories, the Buddha would mention in an offhand way what actions led to rebirth in which realm. The idea of Karma, like reincarnation, was discussed as an accepted fact from which some of his attitudes could be inferred. This makes total sense considering the cultural frame he was working within, where reincarnation was accepted as a fact of life. Hindus believed in reincarnation and for the most part the Buddha's thoughts about reincarnation seem to be mostly Hindu in nature. Certainly the idea of Karma, which we will get into later, is a Hindu idea.

Where the Buddha diverges from Hindu thought and most thought about reincarnation was in the idea of a distinct soul that incarnates over and over again. Remember one of the central concepts of Buddhism is that there is no permanent separate self. The Buddha extended this to include the idea of a soul or spiritual body that moved from one life to another.

In Hindu thought, there is the essence of individuals, which is called an Atman, and it is their belief that this Atman reincarnates over and over again. The Buddha did not support the idea of an Atman, which would imply a permanent spiritual entity as a distinct self. In the Buddha's words, the Atman was also an illusion. As long as you held the illusion of being a distinct individual soul, the effect of reincarnation was the same as the Hindu idea. He taught that what reincarnated was a consciousness that was merely an aggregate of many different conditions and beliefs.

But if there's no self how can there be a self to reincarnate? According to the Buddha, the self that reincarnates is the ego you have created which is ultimately an illusion. When you pierce the illusion of the ego, you also end the cycle of death and rebirth. In the Buddhist view, reincarnation is the result of ignorance. When you are enlightened you no longer create the conditions that lead to rebirth.

So in essence what the Buddha implied, since he never actually said it, is that reincarnation is a fact of life for those who are still lost in ignorance. It exists and yet ultimately it doesn't exist.

It exists to those of us who cannot see the whole picture but this is just another illusion that we must see through in order to liberate ourselves. It is an illusion that leads to yet more suffering than can be encompassed in one short life. It is suffering that will be, for all intents and purposes, eternal until we work to change the conditions that support it.

Why are we discussing something that ultimately doesn't exist? Because in day-to-day reality, most of you reading this book (and even the guy writing this book) are still lost in ignorance. For us, the issue of reincarnation is a fact that must be dealt with in this current condition, since we are still subject to it.

Many Westerners are fairly skeptical of the idea of rebirth. Our Judeo/Christian culture is one in which the idea of survival of the soul after death and an afterlife is seen as a one-shot deal. It does not, however, include an idea of returning to the body. So before we get to discuss the mechanics of reincarnation, I'd like to offer some evidence that you might find persuasive around the idea of reincarnation being a fact of life and death.

Dr. Ian Stevenson

Before I became a Buddhist, I went to grad school for consciousness studies in California (where else?), entering into the world of parapsychology. One of the areas I was most interested in studying, coincidentally, was reincarnation.

In my studies I came across a psychiatrist by the name of Dr. Ian Stevenson who was connected with the University of Virginia in Richmond. He did fascinating work in the area of spontaneous recall of past lives by children. In his landmark book, "Twenty Cases Suggestive of Reincarnation," Stevenson documents cases in and around the world and here in America where young children had spontaneous recall of recent past lives. Typically these cases involved the child remembering extensive details about their former life and eventually when the facts were checked out, found to be amazingly accurate and difficult to explain in any other way than to say they came from an actual memory of a previous birth.

Some of the more interesting cases that Dr. Stevenson studied include one from Texas and one from Turkey. Both of these involve spontaneous recall of past lives by very young children, showing knowledge that is hard to explain any other way than admitting that they were indeed reincarnated. In one case, birthmarks and deformities also highly suggested and lent credence to the idea that the children were having accurate memories of their past lives.

The Case of Walter Miller/Michael Wright

Michael Wright was born in Texas to Catherine Wright in 1975. At around the age of three he began to show some unexpected knowledge of things he should not have known, including the names of people and events he had not personally met or experienced.

He referred to a married friend as Carole Miller, whose married name, and the only name he had ever heard, was Carole Davis. He had only met her twice. Miller was indeed her maiden name, but her name had been Davis for ten years at that point. In the same year he started telling his mother about how he died, which he described in detail. He said his name was Walter Miller and that he died at the age of seventeen in a car crash in 1967. He said, "A friend and I were in a car, and the car went off the road and we rolled over and over. The door came open, and I fell out and was killed." He added that glass in the car had been broken and that his body had been carried over a bridge. He also mentioned the name of the town they were driving back from when the accident occurred.

A newspaper account of the same crash, which occurred in the summer of 1967, verified the details that Michael laid out. There was indeed a Walter Miller who at nearly eighteen years old was killed coming back from a dance with a friend of his. The car went off the road and rolled over. Walter was thrown from the car and was killed instantly when his neck broke. Michael had gotten the name of the town they were driving from correct as well. His body was carried across a bridge to the waiting ambulance.

The most amazing part of this narrative, however, is that Catherine, Michael's mother, knew Walter Miller well. She was engaged to him and was planning to marry him before he was killed. She remembered having a dream when she got pregnant of Walter saying to her in a dream that he was not dead as everyone believed and that he was coming back to her.

Carol Davis whom Michael had called Carol Miller was actually the sister of Walter Miller. He had no way of knowing this when he was three, and yet he did.

When Michael got older, as is typical in many of the cases Dr. Stevenson studied, the memories of his previous life began to fade.

The Case of Semih Tutusmus/Selim Fesli

Two days before Semih Tutusmis's birth his mother had a dream that a man with a bloodied face approached her and told her he had been shot with a shotgun on the right side of his head. He said he wanted to stay with her.

Two days later Semih was born. Oddly, the right side of his face was deformed and his right ear seemed to be missing.

When Semih was a year and a half old he identified the man who had shot him as Isa Kirbekli. He said his own name was Selim Fesli and he named Selims Fesli's wife and the names of all six children. He particularly remembered being shot by Isa Kirbekli and talked about it as if it were not an accident.

On further investigation, it was found that there was indeed a farmer named Selim Fesli, who had been shot by Isa Kirbekli in exactly the manner the little boy had described. Selim had been a farmer from a neighboring village who lay down in his field to rest after a hard day's work. A neighbor hunting rabbits mistook Selim for one in the twilight and shot him on the right side of his head.

Semih also had correctly named the wife and six children of Selim.

When he was less than four years old, he went on his own and walked to the village formerly resided in by Selim. He went right to his erstwhile home and recognized various family members whom he addressed either by name or behaved in such a manner that showed he was familiar with them.

Unlike many of the cases Dr. Stevenson studied, Semih's memories remained strong as he grew. He frequently visited the other village and insisted upon being consulted on important family matters.

At one point he became very upset when a son of Selim's married and he was not invited.

When he heard at one point that another man was courting Selim's wife, Semih went to her and accused her of being unfaithful. He also confronted the man. That must have been awkward.

He continued to hold a grudge against Isa Kerbekli and would throw rocks at the man, threatening him verbally whenever he saw him. Apparently he was convinced that his erstwhile neighbor had not shot him by accident though there was no evidence to back up his claim.

Why These Cases?

I selected these two cases because the one shows that reincarnation memories occur even in places where there is a strong belief to the contrary and social pressure to believe otherwise.

In Texas, Ms. Wright never checked with the friend who had survived the car crash to verify more details that Michael had told her about the night of the crash. She was afraid if word got out about Michael, there would be a serious backlash. Her small Texas town was strongly fundamentalist Christian and not very tolerant of ideas that did not conform to their beliefs.

The second case I chose because of the strong physical evidence as well as the very detailed and lasting memories of the young boy. It is fairly common for Dr. Stevenson to report on cases of spontaneous recall of past lives where the child will have a birthmark or other physical evidence that conforms to a description of the fatal wound taken in the previous life. This case is perhaps the most dramatic example.

These reports are very strong evidence there is something at work here that seems to point to reincarnation.

Other Evidence

There are many books and arguments for and against reincarnation, including the practice of using hypnosis on people to bring them back to memories of past lives.

I myself have undergone this type of hypnosis as part of a study I did in college. I stayed interested and when I was older I trained in its application. I have performed many hypnosis sessions for this purpose. I taught classes on the subject of past lives, and as part of the class I would conduct a group Past Life Hypnosis session. At the end of the session, people were encouraged to share what it was they saw. Often, people in the class who did not know each other in this life would have similar experiences and memories, and realize they were experiencing lives they had shared in the past.

One time when teaching the class, I related one of my own past life histories discovered in hypnosis and a woman sitting in the middle of the class let out a gasp. The life I was relating was my most recent, and involved being shot down during WW II in a bomber over France during the day. As this was a part of my college study, I tried to verify what I had seen in the session and was able to verify that for a very short window of two months in 1944 there was indeed daylight bombing over that section of France. Other than that I had no further evidence, that is, until I found out why this woman had gasped. She was an elderly woman and as it turned out, her husband had been shot down on the very same plane. I was able to verify details with her after the class.

Whether or not the memories uncovered this way are real or just figments of imagination I cannot definitively say. There were some tantalizing occurrences from my study in which I was able to corroborate certain facts from my hypnotic past life recall sessions, but not enough for me to comfortably say it was proof of reincarnation.

That being said, however, I can honestly say that after reading Dr. Stevenson's literature and exploring the matter myself plus learning about some other sources, I am convinced there is some very solid evidence supporting the existence of reincarnation as part of the human experience.

Famous People with Past Life Recall

Some very famous people have had experiences with past life recall, some of these with very distinct memories.

There is the story of General George Patton, who claimed to remember many lives as a warrior. In one famous incident he was being driven to the front in Italy when he ordered the jeep driver to take a turn off at a small dirt road. The road ended up leading to a field containing ancient ruins. Patton then told a story of how he died on that field as a Roman soldier.

In another incident, he said he knew the German army was done for while surveying the aftermath of a battle in

North Africa. He pointed at the abandoned carts on the site of a recent battlefield. The carts reminded him, he said, of the carts that were left behind when Napoleon had been routed at Waterloo. He said he remembered that agonizing retreat, and that the carts were abandoned at that point too.

The novelist Taylor Swift claimed to have memories of a past life as the famous novelist George Sand, who wrote under an assumed male name because it was not acceptable for women to write in those days.

K.D. Laing believes herself to be the reincarnation of famed singer Patsy Cline. Her original band was named K.D. Laing and the Re-Clines.

One of the most interesting cases I am aware of has to do with the Beatle, John Lennon. Once, when visiting Japan and Yoko Ono's family for the first time, he saw a picture of her great grandfather in the place where the ancestors of the family were honored and said in an off-hand way that this was him in a past life.

There were many similarities between Mr. Lennon and the elder Ono family member. For one thing, the great grandfather was described being as close as you could get to being a pop star in 19th century Japan. He was as famous and well-known as the Ex-Beatle had been in this life. The most interesting part of the story, though, comes from Yoko Ono's reaction to John's statement. She was appalled and cautioned John not to say that. Apparently, her great grandfather was shot to death by a disturbed fan.

These are fun and interesting stories to think about, but most importantly they are examples of Westerners having a connection with reincarnation.

Benefit of the Doubt

If after reading these things you still find yourself skeptical about the existence of reincarnation, then welcome to the club. As I said before, despite my own personal experiences and study into the subject, I'm still not completely sold on the idea.

I don't think it is essential for you to believe in reincarnation order to understand its place in Buddhist thought. All I am hoping is for you to give the idea the benefit of the doubt, so that you are open to the possibility of reincarnation. I think with this in mind the rest of what Buddhism has to say will make sense to you.

Perfection

In order to move beyond the need to try to control what is, we need to examine a concept more closely that leads many people astray. It becomes more understandable when looked at through a Buddhist lens. This is the idea of perfection.

I used to teach a class in Reincarnation when I was younger. In every class I would ask the students what they thought was the cause of this continual cycle of death and rebirth. (If you do not believe in reincarnation that's okay, just stick with me through the story. We'll talk about this later). Inevitably one or more people would say that they thought we kept reincarnating until we "got it right." I would then ask them what they meant by getting it right, which always led to my favorite answer.

"We come back until we achieve perfection."

"Great," I would say. "One small question though. What is perfection?"

This is where a silence would fall over the class as they examined for perhaps the first time in their lives what the heck perfection was. It's really hard to find a definition for perfection that is...well...perfect.

It's an important question to answer because the idea of spiritual perfection is so pervasive. Remember, "perfect" is not the same as good or good enough. Perfection is an absolute. There can be no caveats or exceptions when defining perfection.

So what is perfection? Take a minute and see if you can come up with a definition for perfection that is absolutely perfect. Not that easy, right? And yet, a true definition of this word that we use so often and casually is essential if we are to answer the question, what are we doing here?

Try this one on for size:

Perfection is
When something is
Exactly
What it is.

Let that sink in. You may want to reread that definition a few times. Perfection is when something is exactly what it is.

Let's say for example that this morning I prevented a small child from being run over by a car. It seems that would be the perfect thing to do in that situation. But now years pass and the child grows up to be the next Hitler. Now the idea of perfection gets a little hazier.

The fact is you cannot understand what is Perfection without being able to see all the ramifications. You would need to be omniscient and omnipresent in order to judge truly.

This definition implies a complete trust and faith in what is present. It encompasses the laws of dependent co-arising, no self, emptiness and impermanence as well. It accepts that whatever it is that has manifested in the present moment has done so because the entire universe supports its manifestation at this moment. If you trust that the universe is a beneficent force based in eternal love, it is impossible for anything that is not perfect to manifest. We may not get it or appreciate it, but its presence is absolutely and without equivocation perfect.

This is also why avoidance creates suffering. Often the greatest gifts and our greatest teachers come from situations we would classify as negative. Often we seek to avoid certain situations, because on a very basic level we understand that it is something that threatens to wake us up and cause us to face something we have not been willing to face.

So if this is the case then we are already perfect at every point in our journey. So perfection cannot explain why we would reincarnate.

> *Perfection is*
> *When something is*
> *Exactly*
> *What it is.*
>   *- Me*

Is the Universe Unfair and Cruel?

This is an important point to consider when attempting the understanding of the mechanics of reincarnation.

Why is it that some people are born to wealth and health and seem to live a charmed life while others are born in poverty with broken bodies and broken spirits? Can the Universe be so Cruel and uncaring as to allow for this randomness to occur? If this is indeed the only life it would seem this Universe is a very unfair place to live.

Only in reincarnation can we understand that each person is born into the situation that provides the right environment for him or her to learn the lessons they need to learn. We'll discuss this in greater detail later.

The Mechanics of Buddhist Rebirth

The cycle of Rebirth consists of Birth, Death, and Rebirth and continues for as long as it takes us to attain enlightenment, at which point we need never return again.

The Buddha said that anything that is born would die. Put another way, anything, which has a starting point, has an ending point. The end of life as we see it is certainly the end of this chapter of life, but it is a transitional state that eventually becomes the starting point for the next life. The fear we experience about death, which permeates so much of what we do, is based on the ignorance of the continuity of life through the cycles of rebirth and beyond. Death is *an* end, not *the* end. It is an end of a chapter not the end of the book.

When we are reborn, the conditions of the new life are set by the actions we have taken during the previous lives. We create the conditions that become the challenges and opportunities that we meet in our current life. Simply put, if you do a lot of good then your next life will be filled with a lot of good. If you do a lot of bad, you will be reborn into difficult circumstances. That's a very simple way of putting it and in fact it's a bit more complicated than that. But that gives you the essence of the thing.

Do good, good returns to you. Do bad and it will return to you as well.

If there are things you fear and avoid, you can bet you will meet them again in this and future lives until you reach a point where you find an appreciation for them. Remember avoidance is a form of clinging. Those, which we fear and resist, are the very things that through our lives will persist. (I rhymed!)

Of course, those things we desire and cling to will return to us as well, keeping us in the cycle of rebirth until we begin to see these things not as special possessions but as impermanent manifestations no better and no worse than everything else.

According to the Buddha, we have right up until the moment of our deaths to find this truth and realize it in order to free ourselves. For this very reason, Buddhists spend an awful lot of time thinking about death and how to transition in a skillful manner.

The end of the cycle of rebirth is the Holy Grail of Buddhism. The Buddha said that his life as the Buddha was the end of the cycle for him. When you end the cycle you are said to be in Nirvana. To understand how this works we need to delve into the idea of Karma.

Karma

Karma is one of the most well-known and yet most misunderstood sanskrit words to have made it into

Western consciousness. I have heard Karma being used as meaning a form of divine punishment for past misdeeds or rewards for past good deeds. In a very basic sense these are understandable mischaracterizations.

The action of Karma is a profound and subtle force that must be understood on a deeper level to be fully appreciated.

Karma is a sanskrit word which translates literally as "action." It is a force that comes into play whenever an action is taken. It's the spiritual equivalent of Newton's Law of Motion which states, "for every action there is an equal and opposite reaction."

It is the balancing property of the Yin Yang at work in the world. Movement in one direction of the wheel necessarily causes movement of the rest of the wheel. The Universe must restore harmony when any attempt or action causes the balance to shift to one side of the wheel. When this is the case the Universe acts to recreate a balance.

Another way of looking at it is to imagine a completely still, smooth surface of a pond. This is representative of our Buddha Nature. Buddha Nature moves in harmony with all that there is, so on the surface of the pond no disturbance is created that would roil the water. When, however, we act in a way that is not in accord with our True Nature, we are going against the flow of the universe and creating countercurrents that leave the universe to apply a countervailing force in order to smooth the pond to its natural undisturbed and peaceful state.

When you move in accord with your Buddha Nature you have done nothing at this point to create Karma. Then you do something that is against your Nature, and it is like a rock is being dropped into the center of the completely still pond. That one act causes ripples that quickly spread in all directions, meet the shore and rebound back toward the spot of the first action. So your actions have consequences that do not disappear somewhere out there but return to you.

In this respect, if you do something with evil intent, the evil will come back to you. The same is true of well-intentioned acts. So it would seem that the idea of cosmic reward and punishment is indeed the definition of Karma. But let's look more deeply.

Another way of looking at it is that any action plants a seed. When you do something you know in your heart to be wrong, it is like planting the seed of a thorn bush. At any time you could repent for your deed and try to make amends thereby balancing the evil act with a good one. In the arena of Karma, intention is everything. If, however, you refuse to repent or even admit that the act you committed was, to use the Buddhist term, unskillful, it is like sitting on the spot where you planted the seed and staying rooted there. At first this will not be uncomfortable but as the seed begins to grow and the thorns break the soil, the painful consequences of your act will manifest under you.

Evil acts require a trunkful of excuses, reasons, and justifications. Honorable acts travel light. Nobody sees himself or herself as doing evil, so it may be hard to tell if what you are doing is creating good or bad Karma. One simple test is found in the words above. If you feel yourself needing to justify an act, or excuse it, or count reasons and a full narrative for why it was really not a bad thing to do, you can bet your bippie (how's that for an archaic turn of phrase?) you're doing something wrong and creating more suffering for others and for yourself.

To continue the seed analogy, you cannot grow an apple tree from a briar seed. If you plant thorns, thorns will grow and will create suffering. If you plant an apple seed a fruit tree will grow which will provide sustenance for yourself and others.

So again, it still sounds like good deeds are rewarded and bad deeds are punished. The key to understanding this is in replacing the words reward and punishment with needed lessons.

In order to free ourselves from suffering, we must overcome our ignorance. Karma is designed to be the greatest instructor of all. We set the lessons by our own actions, which, by the way, do indeed speak louder than words. If I am ignorant of beauty in the world I am going to act in a very ugly manner toward it, which will return ugliness to me as a matter of course, thereby strengthening my belief that the world is an evil place.

When I have experienced the action of this ugliness myself (not a pleasant experience) I will begin to feel wrong about committing this ugliness on anyone else. In other words, I will develop compassion. This process may take a very long time for some people who are especially attached to their ways of seeing the world. Eventually even the hardest cases "get" it.

Conversely, when I commit acts of kindness and generosity and they are returned to me, I understand in a very deep way what kindness and generosity adds to the world. I end up wanting to see more of it so I act accordingly, thereby freeing myself more and more.

Buddhism has an alternative way to look at good and evil that I find very useful. The terms "skillful" and "unskillful" are used in place of good, bad, righteous, evil, etc. The idea is that ultimately you would like whatever you do to be working towards your eventual liberation from suffering. Therefore, the question you must ask yourself before you act (and before you speak, and even when looking at what you think), is whether this is a skillful means by which I am promoting my liberation, or is it an unskillful means by which I am burying myself deeper in the cycle of suffering?

Of course, with compassion the same question must be applied to how your acts affect others as well. Generally speaking, skillful means will bring about Karmic consequences that will be an aid to your path of liberation. Unskillful means will cause your path to become muddied.

The way Karma works is similar to how we get ourselves stuck here in the cycle of rebirth. Again, the significant agent is desire. When I am attached to something it causes me to behave in a certain way that is all about attaining this particular thing. There is no way to cling and act in this way that does not cause ripples on the pond, so to speak. It is against our True nature, which is like the calm and undisturbed surface of the pond.

When we flow and move in exact harmonious ways directed by the currents and flows within the pond, we do not create any disturbance. It is only when we fight the current to go off in a direction of our own choosing that we create ripples and disturbances on the surface, which in turn causes Karma to come into play.

Therefore the best way to act is to do so in the knowledge that what you do at this precise moment is going to come back to you. You can consciously choose to create something wonderful in every moment or some future grief. The choice is entirely yours.

The Key Is Compassion

Our True nature is one of an infinite well of compassion and kindness. When we act in this manner and hold this in our hearts we do not create Karma. When we do not create Karma we free ourselves from the Cycle of Rebirth. When we are free of the cycle of rebirth, that's where the fun really begins.

So Karma is not a form of cosmic punishment but a force of ultimate compassion. It is the method by which we learn lessons of compassion. It is not a problem to be conquered but a series of lessons that will work to free us in the end by teaching us the same big lesson over and over until we get it.

The intensity of the correction exactly matches the condition of our own minds when performing actions in the world. We set the course of our future, and our future lives. This means we are now living through the lessons we have set for ourselves in the past. How we deal with it now will determine whether or not we are ready to move on from this lesson, or need to meet it again. If we meet whatever comes with equanimity and grace, we release the need to meet it again. If we resist or try to hold on to it we are just creating more Karma. We dispel Karma through acceptance and grace and we practice acceptance and grace when we meditate.

Our lesson in this life is to learn to see the beauty of all manifestations, to see through the form straight to the manifestation of the Dharma within. When we can treat everything with equanimity and compassion Karma has done its work and saved us from our cycle of suffering.

The Cycle of Suffering

The Cycle of Rebirth is referred to in Buddhism as the Cycle of Suffering, as the mechanics and force behind the two are identical. Desire and ignorance lead to clinging and avoiding, which create the forces that keep us continually suffering until we learn to let them be what they are. That's all we have to do to end the cycle. Let go of what we think things should be by accepting what things are.

The answer is indeed simple. If you understand the Four Noble Truths and follow the Noble Eightfold Path, you will let go of all that causes you to suffer and end suffering forever.

Like many aspects of Buddhism, it is simple, but it is not easy.

Why, when the answer is so simple, do we perpetuate the very things that cause us to suffer? The Buddha understood that intellectual understanding of the problem was not enough. He knew that no matter how eloquently he spoke, no matter what words he used, unless a person learned these lessons through their own direct experience it would make no difference.

Someone can tell you that fire is hot and should be avoided, but until you experience being burned this is only a one-dimensional understanding once removed from your own mind and heart.

If we have not experienced the Truth of the Buddhist path then our understanding of it is only superficial. You are being asked to take something on faith because somebody else told you it was true. This is not going to be enough to get you to commit to changing almost everything about yourself in order to find freedom. That type of commitment requires knowing, not just believing.

We are creatures of habit. We tend to do things the same way over and over again until we actually grow neural pathways in our brain that cause us to act in the same ways without any conscious thought. Trying to go against these deeply ingrained behaviors requires a great deal of effort and discipline as well as constant vigilance.

Unless we live each and every moment in a mindful state and consciously choose our actions, we will relapse into the well-worn ruts we have created over years of traveling the same path. To do anything requiring this much constant attention and vigilance, we must have a deep desire to do so.

What Keeps Us Returning?

Passion feeds desire, and desire is the motivating energy that moves the universe. This is not to say that desire is a bad thing. On the contrary, without the strong desire to be free there would be no hope of ever escaping the cycle of suffering.

What we need to understand is that desire is a powerful force. If it's not directed in a mindful and purposeful manner, it will bring about situations that will have painful consequences.

You move toward that which you desire, and even draw to yourself those things that you avoid, through a use of negative desire, which still has an attractive force to it.

Basically, without understanding the power of the force we are employing, we create the circumstances that form the basis for all the conditions of our lives, including the semi-conscious choice to continue the cycle of rebirth.

You will be drawn to and attract that which you desire. If, at the time of your exit from this world you still desire anything of it, you will return. That in itself is the cause of rebirth. When you transcend these desires and learn to use desire in a skillful manner, directed toward liberation, you are free to move on.

Freedom from the Cycle of Suffering

So in the process of living and dying and being reborn we get to learn by direct experience what it is that liberates us and what things cause us to remain in the whirlpool of rebirth.

Understanding is the key. We must study our own lives and begin to see where we are attached and where the path to freedom lies.

Clinging and Avoiding

Clinging and avoiding come from not understanding the nature of reality. The Buddha said, "All the dharmas are empty." What did he mean by this? What are they empty of? How can everything be empty when they seem so real?

The dharmas, in this case, means all of the manifestations one finds on the earth, as well as all of the lessons of all the manifestations one finds on the earth. The idea is that although there appear to be many dharmas, there is really only one. All things contain Buddha Nature, and Buddha Nature is the one unchanging thing in the Universe.

All things are not separate entities or even distinct from each other. They differ only in form, but in essence they are the same as everything else.

By mistakenly seeing one thing as special over another, we create an illusion about that object that spins a web of illusion around it and anchors us to it. We think some things are good and other things are bad. Furthermore, we think we need to hold on to good things and avoid bad things.

The fact is that all good things have elements of bad in them, and all bad things have elements of good as well, even if we have not learned to see and appreciate that fact. It causes us to lose equanimity as we meet what we consider to be good or bad. When good happens we get high, and when bad happens we get low. The appropriate reaction to all things is a form of neutral appreciation and acceptance of the oneness of all things. Only when we understand this can we stop clinging and avoiding. Only then can we free ourselves.

The dharmas are empty of separate selves. They are one. None of them is more special than any other. All of them contain Buddha Nature; therefore they are all equally special. So the idea of valuing one thing over another, or one state of being over another is a form of ignorance of the Truth of the emptiness of the dharmas.

The Awakened One

The Buddha means "the Awakened One." Awakening is the thing we must achieve in order to free ourselves. But awaken from what? Where is the dream we are dreaming from which we must awaken? What if the regular everyday life that we lead is nothing more than a dream? We discussed this earlier but it bears repeating because it is so important. What if when we go to sleep or pass on we are actually waking from a dream? What is the significance of dreaming and awakening?

We live lives of illusion and miss the incredible reality that exists in every present moment. We actually call extreme examples of this "daydreaming," but the fact is we are always daydreaming when we are not absolutely present in the present moment. Our minds drift and we go on trips of fantasy that end up becoming more real to us than what is actual at the moment. We use cameras to take pictures of "special" moments so that we can relive them, but the fact is that our attention was on the camera at the time and not in the moment at all. So, in point if fact, we never actually experienced that moment in the first place.

We look at pictures of ourselves and place value upon how we appear, and who we were with, and what was happening. We even identify enough to dredge up a memory about that moment. The fact remains that who we are at the distinct moment when we are looking at the photo is not the same person that is pictured in the photo.

Our cells are constantly dying and being reborn. Our thoughts and emotions are fluid as we age from one moment to the next. What we are seeing when we look at that photo is something which does not exist anymore. We are looking at an illusion meant to represent the past, but all we are truly seeing are the light rays that have gone through a lens and been digitally recorded into binary code to reconstruct a symbol of what was present at that time. There's an infinite amount of information not recorded in that photo, and so the best photo of all only represents an infinitesimal fraction of the moment in question.

But who thinks this way? Usually we do the shortcut thinking, allowing ourselves to believe we are seeing a picture of the actual past as it actually happened. If we look a little more deeply, we can understand that it is nothing of the sort. The same reasoning we applied to our names applies here as well. Just as we have no names, there is no past in the present moment.

Conscious memories are just like photos in that way. We say we remember something just as it was but it doesn't take long to discover that anyone else who happened to be in the same place had a very different experience and a very different memory than we do. The only thing we can truly say about the past is that it is past and therefore does not exist. Yet, we hold on to our photos and our memories and our longings for the simpler times we recall so clearly.

The same can be said about projections of the future. One can plan and scheme and seek to control all of creation so as to force a certain outcome. But what one often finds is that after all that effort and sweat and tears, the future they brought about is not what they thought it would be.

In fact, the future does not exist. When you arrive there you are still in the present moment, a fully real and tangible place as opposed to the phantoms of the past and the future. Yet how many of us live fully in the present moment?

Guilt is a creature of the past just as fear is a creation that lives in the future. Neither one has any reality or power to hurt you or make you suffer, yet how many of us do indeed suffer from guilt and fear?

This is the dream state we live in, where our fears and guilt seem to have tangible form and separate selves that seek to punish us or make us want to run away and hide. These are the nightmares we conjure up while we remain in darkness with our ignorance.

The good news is that just as with the nightmares we have at night, there is an ending and a waking that frees us from them. Just as the waking up dispels the experience of the nightmare, so too, the Waking Up dispels all of the fears and guilts and goblins we have lived with and thought were so real.

Dreaming and Waking States

In order to understand the nature of reality, we have to look at things a little differently. We tend to think of the moment of birth as the first moment of life, when it is actually the experience of closing down much of our consciousness, allowing it to focus into a very narrow perspective.

At birth, we change from an eternal immortal omnipotent divine being to a helpless mortal creature whose consciousness is severely limited. Birth is actually the moment of the beginning of a new dream.

What follows, for as many years as this body lasts in this world, is the continuation of that dream. How we dream and what we do with the symbols we meet in the dream are significant in the process of our evolution towards enlightenment. We can choose to live these lives with eyes straight ahead, never looking left nor right nor up nor down and have a very narrow and limited experience. Or we can treat this life as an opportunity to explore the dream and see what we can learn.

When we meditate, what we are actually doing is training ourselves to dream in a lucid fashion. Lucid dreaming is a skill some seek to acquire that allows them to have some control and consciousness while they sleep. In the same way, we meditate in order to learn how we can learn to steer the dream and more importantly, allow our consciousness to take part in the experience.

The ultimate goal is to be awake while in the dream. This is what the Buddha achieved and why he was called the Awakened One.

Sooner or later we all do wake from the dream as we pass from this life. Depending on how we have lived this dream we either remain awake or eventually go back to sleep to experience yet another dream. If we go back to sleep after life we are going back into a dream. We experience this as reincarnation or rebirth. Just as with our dreams when we sleep, the dreams we have when we are reborn are conditioned by who and what we see ourselves to be and will include those things to which we are attached in one way or another.

We keep repeating this cycle until we can become fully awake within the dream. Then we are free and can go on to live a fully Awakened existence at the end. This is called Nirvana.

The Actor's Occupational Hazard

So if all of this is true, and it's that simple to return to our True Nature and free ourselves from suffering, why don't we just do it? How do we get stuck in this cycle of rebirth?

Look at it this way. When we incarnate we create a new character in much the same way an actor does when creating a new role in a play. Any actor worth his salt works hard to commit so strongly to the role that while the play is on, he is "lost" in that role.

He actually becomes the character he is playing. Afterwards when the play is over and the actor goes backstage and gets to remove the makeup and costume, he drops the character along with the trappings.

But there is an occupational hazard for any actor and that is that the role they play will become so deeply ingrained that they have difficulty dropping the character after the show ends. They develop an attachment to the character and even see the character as a distinct and real individual. Taken to the extreme, the actor could lose himself completely in the role and not be able to drop it after the show, becoming stuck in that role beyond the life of the play.

This is a metaphor for what has happened to us and why we keep coming back to be born again and again. There is a desire and a deeply held attachment to things that were never meant to be more than props in a play.

All suffering comes from this case of mistaken identity. We are not who we think we are.

We chase wealth, power and fame, seeking to glorify these characters we have created. Some are willing to do terrible things in order to imbue these characters with things that they hope will give them life beyond the scope of the play. Of course all of these exertions are futile in the end, serving only to increase the pain and suffering of others and ourselves, but in the context of the play they seem to make perfect sense.

In order to end this cycle of insanity we must be able to see that it is just a play, that these roles are temporary, and that there is a greater existence for us beyond playing this one character on this one small stage.

Conquering Death

When you can see the end of the play as simply "the end of the play," it no longer holds any dread for you. As an actor I can tell you that I love being on stage. I feel a little sad when the run of a play ends. You tend to get very close with your fellow actors and share a bond with them, even though in many cases you may not know the actors themselves nearly as well or intimately as you have known their characters. Inevitably, though, the end comes. The scenery is broken down and stored, the props and costumes are put away, and the lines you have worked so hard to memorize begin to fade from memory. Life outside of the theater returns in all of its beautiful randomness and richness. You still love the characters and the actors and the experience, but you are also glad to be going home and looking forward to your next project.

Imagine looking at life and death in this way. If death is synonymous with ending a role we have performed so that we can return to our own life does that really sound scary?

We have a fairly extensive body of reports from people who have had near death experiences. Generally they report having been met with family and loved ones that have passed before them welcoming them. They talk about feelings of calm and peace and warmth, and a being of light that filled them with a feeling of unconditional love. Doesn't sound very scary either, does it? It sounds like going home after the play.

Sooner or later we will all go through the experience and find out for ourselves what awaits us, but so far in everything I have read and experienced I am fairly certain that death is no more to be feared than going home after a long hard day of work and finally getting to take off your shoes and put your feet up.

The cycle of rebirth is ubiquitous. Everyone who is alive today was born and will die and will be reborn again in a continuous cycle. We start the process of dying the moment we are born and we start the process of birth the moment we die. Everything is always in a constant state of movement and change.

How can we square this reality with our obsession for security? Change produces a great deal of stress and anxiety in those who feel they need security and certainty. Change comes to be seen as a form of death and the same terror buttons gets pushed. It seems like a terrible joke to play on us that we are born only to die.

What compassionate G-d would create such a thing? Why would we fall in love only to be certain of separation from that person? Why are we born with a talent which burns bright as we grow but burns out as we age?

Remember the cycles of the sun and the cycles of the season, which mirror the cycles of rebirth. Death is *AN* end, not *THE* end. This end is also the beginning. Just as in the Yin Yang you cannot have one without the other. There is no such thing as a final end.

No Fear

When we understand this Truth we are free from the worst fear of all. There is no more reason to fear death than there is to fear waking up, or winter, or night time, or the end of a play or any other part of any process that occurs in nature.

When we start to appreciate this truth we begin to understand that all of our fears are ridiculous and unfounded and based upon ignorance. We begin to feel lighter as we're freed from our greatest fear and the source of so much suffering. We can stop worrying about the future and regretting the past and begin to actually live in the present.

Transcending the Cycle

When you have done enough work on the Noble Eightfold Path, you will find yourself being fully compassionate with everything. When you are fully compassionate with everything, you will develop an equanimity that cannot be shaken by unforeseen events. You understand that everything that exists and everything that occurs has only one lesson for you. All the dharmas are empty. They are all the same. Nothing is any more or less special than anything else. When you lose one thing you are still surrounded by everything else. Everything has the same seed, the same Buddha Nature; therefore you realize you have actually lost nothing.

It is only the ego that experiences and fears death. Our True nature is immortal and has no reason to fear anything. It recognizes that though there may be sadness associated with an ending, that same moment brings with it anticipation of something new and wonderful that is arising at the same time.

This is the work we do in meditation. When we practice meditation we begin to see deeply into the True nature of everything and most especially ourselves.

When you reach this point, you will experience here as being the same as there, and this being just like that, and that everything has the same seed and it is a thing of joy and beauty. You are at peace and at one with all that exists because this very same seed is what you are finding in yourself as well.

Summarizing

Birth, Death and Rebirth are Inseparable

Remember Yin/Yang and that all opposites are not two distinct and separate things but two sides of the same coin. The sides are inseparable. This is true of the process of birth and death as well. Whatever is born will die and whatever dies will be born, only to die again and be reborn and on and on.

The Cycle of Birth Death Rebirth

We come back again and again, born into different bodies and living multiple lifetimes in an attempt to free ourselves from this cycle in which we are stuck. We suffer the occupational hazard of actors as we get lost in our roles and forget that we are merely actors playing a part. When we remember who and what we really are we can free ourselves.

Karma is the Key

Karma, a sanskrit word meaning action, is not a form of divine punishment but is the force by which we meet what we put out into the world. We plant a seed and the Karma is the fruit of that plant. If we consciously plant a seed that is good we will enjoy the fruits of our action. If we plant a seed that is a cause of suffering, we will experience the thorny bush that grows as a result. Karma holds the key to learning what we need to learn to free ourselves. Through it we set the lessons we need to learn. By acting always in accord with our own True nature of Love we create no Karma.

Passions/Desires set Life Conditions

What you are passionate about, what you desire most, is what you will move toward. Avoidance is just another form of desire and it has the attractive property as well. You will meet what you desire and the strength of your passion around that desire will determine the severity of the lesson you are setting up for yourself. If you desire something or things in this world you will return. Likewise, a passion or desire for freedom from suffering is important for those setting out on the path to liberation.

Dreaming/Awakening/Sleeping

Life is a dream that we dream while we sleep in the spiritual sense. When we can learn to awaken from the dream we free ourselves from the cycle of dreaming. Dying is the process of temporarily awakening from one dream before we go back to sleep and dream a new dream, which is rebirth.

No Fear of Closing Doors

Remember that a door closing means that another one is opening right behind you. Don't waste your time and energy pounding on closed doors. Turn around and walk through the open door and you will find new adventures, beauty and joy.

Transcend the Cycle

Remember that your ultimate goal is to transcend the cycle of rebirth and become totally awake within the dream. Your goal is to become a Buddha and an Awakened One. Eventually we will all revert to our True nature and become Buddhas. How long we spend being less than we truly are is entirely up to us. The way has been pointed out to us and that, in a nutshell, is Buddhism.

But there is a little more. At the beginning of the book I promised you that I would explain the title of this book. Read on!

PART 2

Kill the Buddha

CHAPTER 7
Meet The Buddha Kill The Buddha

Crossing the River

Once there was a young man who set out to find Nirvana. He wandered far and wide and everywhere he went he would seek out the religious representatives or the authorities or study some sacred scripture but always his search was in vain.

Then one day he happened upon a village that was situated by the banks of a wide river. Everyone he asked at that village gave the same answer. "Nirvana? Why it is right across that river and up over the ridge." This was the first time he had such a definitive answer.

Enthusiastically he went down to the river and searched for a way across but there did not seem to be any way to cross it. It was too wide to swim and there was no ferry or bridge to cross either. He picked a direction and began to explore the near bank. He was looking for a shallow place or a place where the river narrowed but search as he might he could find no easy crossing.

He was so close to his goal and yet it still eluded him. Finally just as he was about to give up and go the other way he came upon a small hut with a beautiful boat leaning up against it. The boat was covered in engravings and gold and looked like the work of a master Boatwright.

There was an old man sitting at the entrance to this hut so he approached him. "Sir," he said. "Would you be so kind as to carry me across the river in your fine boat?"

The old man demurred. "This boat as you can see is built to carry only one person."

"In that case, sir, would you be willing to sell me the boat in return for services I could render?"

Again the old man answered in the negative. "Look at this boat carefully you will see it is carved with the greatest care and artistry. I am a master Boatwright and this is my crowning creation. I will not sell it. However since you have offered to work for me I would suggest you work for yourself under my tutelage and I will instruct you and train you in how to build such a work of art for yourself. Then you will have a boat in order to cross the river."

Immediately the young man accepted the old man's offer and sat down beside him to begin his lessons. The old man taught him how to find the best wood and then how to painstakingly carve that wood. After the general shape of the boat was formed he then instructed the young man in how to find paints and stain in order to decorate the boat properly as well as how to carve details into it.

After one year the boat was finished and it was a masterpiece. The young man was very proud of it. He bid the old man goodbye and thanked him as he launched his boat into the river and prepared to cross.

When he reached the other side he carried his boat onto the shore and made sure it would not float away. He began to climb the ridge but as he walked away he found that he could not leave behind the boat he had worked so hard and so long to build. So he returned to the river and put the boat upon his back.

When he reached the crest of the ridge he spied before him a magnificent golden palace and knew at once that he had finally found Nirvana. With his boat upon his back he walked to the entrance to the palace grounds but it turned out that it was a narrow gate and no matter how he turned and angled it he could not fit through with the boat. He was so close to his life's goal but he still found that he could not bear to part with the boat.

He looked around and decided that this area outside of the palace was very pleasant and since he was at least close to Nirvana maybe he could live out here instead of going in. He walked around the palace wall and when he turned the corner he saw before him hundreds and thousands of people camped out there all with their own boats.

At that point he realized his error and dropped the boat to the ground so that he could enter the gates. He now lives in Nirvana and has never regretted his choice.

Meet The Buddha

The other chapters of this book all have to do with meeting the Buddha. As I promised you in the introduction however, I was going to explain the strange title and so far I have explained half the title. You have been introduced to the Buddha. In order to really meet the Buddha you have some work to do applying what you have learned in the front section of this book.

From His life story you can recognize the Nature of the Buddha and see just how his story is actually your story as well. The path he walked is the path we must all walk someday. It is a metaphor for how to walk the spiritual path with great devotion and intention.

Study and come to see deeply into the Four Noble Truths and the Noble Eightfold Path to find your own way to liberation from suffering and to a joyful life.

Look for signs of Impermanence, Dependent Co-Arising and Emptiness of a separate self in everything.

Begin to discipline yourself to create a robust meditation practice for yourself so that you can deepen your insight and lighten your load.

Look deeply into the nature of birth, death and rebirth not only for yourself but also in all of nature wherever you may find it. Use this direct experience to transcend fear and fully live your Buddha Nature.

When you do these things you will meet the Buddha in a deep and profound way. But understand that I am not just talking about meeting Shakyamuni Buddha whose story was told in the first chapter of this book. When you hear someone speak of the Buddha they are generally talking about this man who lived 2600 years ago and who is the founder of modern Buddhism. But the Buddha I am talking about here is something different.

Where is the Buddha? Who is the Buddha? Where is the greatest spiritual master you can find? Where are all the answers to the profound questions of the Universe? Look no further than in your own heart and mind. Understand I am talking about meeting the latent Buddha within yourself. When you have developed a loving heart that beats to the rhythm of Your True nature and a mind that is disciplined and sees deeply into the Truth of the universe. That is when you truly meet the Buddha.

Yes, And...?

So having answered what was intended in the first half of the title I will now try to explain the second and perhaps more confusing part of the title, Kill The Buddha. I think you can see from the rest of this book that I love Buddhism and treasure it. I am so grateful to the Buddha for all of his lessons that have helped so many others and me as well. So why would I write a book about killing the Buddha?

The Buddha once said, "Do not mistake the finger pointing at the moon for the moon itself." What he was cautioning his listeners about was that they should not worship him as a god or a mystical being. They should not get caught up in rituals and relics and dead scriptures. He was interested in creating a religion only insofar as it provided a vehicle to train people to achieve liberation. Just as he was laser focused when he taught, he was just as focused in what he wanted to leave as a legacy to those who would follow the path.

This is a common problem for those who have founded religions. Before long what they teach is subjugated to the fetishizing of "sacred relics" and magical words of power. The synagogue I attended as a child performed all of the services in Hebrew, and I assure you, 99.9% of the people attending had no inkling of the meaning. But it seemed sacrilegious to consider doing it any other way. My family were conservative Jews and that's the way services are performed in most Jewish sects. Only in the reformed Jewish tradition are the services performed in English. Because of this, other Jews look down upon them. I myself attended some reformed services and felt a lot was missing. I understand the tradition and ritualization that attends religious ceremony. But this very thing was what the Buddha warned against when he made that statement about the moon.

In the 9th Century a Zen Master by the name of Lin Chi, offered a famous koan. Lin Chi was the founder of the Rinzai sect of Zen Buddhism, a part of Zen that uses paradoxical statements and questions (called koans) that cannot be answered except through direct experience of the Truth. Some koans you may have heard: "If a tree falls in the forest and there is no one to hear it, does it make a sound?" or "What is the sound of one hand clapping?"

The koan that directly influenced the name of this book is also quite well known though not usually understood. "If you meet the Buddha on the road, kill him."

If you are looking for the Buddha you will not find him outside of yourself. If you are traveling on a road going hither and yon to find what is inside of yourself, whatever you find out there may seem sacred and you may be tempted to worship it, put it on a pedestal, but it is not the Buddha. It is a golden calf, a graven image, an idol and an illusion. So if you are on the road and you think you have found the Buddha, Lin Chi suggests that you metaphorically kill it. Dispose of it so that your vision is not occluded or it will prevent you from finding the True Buddha in yourself.

The Buddha once said that religion is like a raft. When attempting to cross from the bank of suffering across the river to the bank of liberation a raft is necessary. But he said it would be foolish to continue to carry the raft once you had crossed. It would weigh you down and slow your progress, eventually making you subject to exhaustion just at the time when you need all of your energy focused to achieve final liberation.

Great teaching leads you to the brink. It is like a good map that shows you the way. You would not make offerings or sacrifices to the map though. That would just be silly.

The signs and portents and lessons and disciplines, the practice and the guiding, have all led you to this place where you are ready to cross over into freedom.

Freedom means freedom from everything. If there is something you are clinging to, you are not free. So at this point it is entirely appropriate to let go – even of those things you have held as sacred. Great teaching leads you to the brink, but you must walk to final stretch on your own two feet.

You Meet The Buddha and Kill The Buddha when you realize that you are the Buddha. (Even in New Jersey.)

The Kalama Sutra

This Sutra (or lesson) is known as the Buddha's charter of free inquiry, and it contains, what is in my opinion, the most important teaching of the Buddha. This is what I feel sets Buddhism apart from other traditions and religions. I studied and participated in other religions before I found my home in Buddhism, and each one contained great Truths. Where I had trouble with those other religions was where it became clear to me that in order to be a member or participate you had to uncritically accept certain ideas on faith, surrendering your own judgment and common sense in the exchange. That just never sat right with me.

The story of the Kalama Sutra takes place in a village the Buddha was passing through called Kesaputta. Upon seeing the Buddha the people of the village explained to him that many teachers of other traditions had passed through their village recently and shared their teachings with the inhabitants. The people were confused because every teacher was very adamant that only their teaching was correct and criticized other teachings as being mistaken.

The people asked the Buddha how could they know for sure that one teaching is truer than another when there are so many. The Buddha's response is the Kalama Sutra.

> Do not believe in something because it is reported. Do not believe in something because it has been practiced by generations or becomes a tradition or part of a culture. Do not believe in something because a scripture says it is so. Do not believe in something believing a god has inspired it. Do not believe in something a teacher tells you to. Do not believe in something because the authorities say it is so. Do not believe in hearsay, rumor, speculative opinion, public opinion, or mere acceptance to logic and inference alone. Help yourself, accept as completely true only that which is praised by the wise and which you test for yourself and know to be good for yourself and others.

Isn't that an amazing thing for the founder of a religion to say? He says we should listen to those we know to be wise certainly but then goes on to say that whatever you hear you must filter through your own heart. It implies a great trust in our own ability to be able to distinguish between what is and is not true. It says that the Truth resides in our own hearts and that this is the final arbiter of what is true and what is not.

On my first weekend at a monastery, during one of the sitting periods, students were given the chance to have a private meeting with the abbot. Waiting my turn when the bell rung I went into the cell where the abbot sat. I bowed three times and asked my question.

"Sir, I have been searching for spiritual truth for what feels like a long time. Though I have found truth in all religions I seem to have a problem being able to fully commit to one. I guess I just don't fit well with organized religion."

In response he said, "You are your own Guru." And rang the bell indicating that the interview was over and that it was time for me to leave.

I'd like to say that his words immediately opened up my eyes to new vistas of possibilities and set me on the right path from then on. In actuality my inner response was more like, "That's it? I'm my own guru? That's what I waited and bowed to hear?"

I did not fully get it at the time, but as the years passed I have come to understand how profound and significant these words were.

The fact is that everyone is his or her own guru. The place to go to find the Buddha is within your own body and heart. May you find him soon and live joyfully ever after.

I bow to the Buddha in you.

BUDDHIST GLOSSARY

Ahimsa - The principle of non-violence. Buddhists revere all forms of life as sentient beings and seek to treat every sentient being with reverence and compassion. One of the Buddhist vows is that we will save all sentient beings. To harm any sentient being is to harm ourselves.

Arhat - One who has attained enlightenment.

Atman & Anatman- Atman is a Hindu concept of a separate spirit or soul of an individual self which survives from incarnation to incarnation. Anatman is the absence of such a soul or self and is more in tune with the teaching of the Buddha.

Bardo - According to the Tibetan Book Of The Dead there are four stages in the cycle of birth and rebirth. Each of these stages is a bardo. The four bardos are; becoming, life, dissolution or death and the between life state of pure consciousness.

Bikkhu - Literally this means "beggar." It is the term that the Buddha applied to all who became monks and is used in that context within Buddhism. A Bikkhu is one who has renounced the earthly attachments and become a monk who supports himself through begging. In the Buddha's time, his monks were given a bowl and went every day to the village to beg for food for that day. In return they would offer lessons and blessings. This was the Buddha's way of ensuring that monks would remain connected to the lay people and the teaching would be shared.

Bikkhuni - As with bikkhu but for a female. A bikkhuni is a nun. At first the Buddha resisted ordaining or accepting females into his monasteries as the social evolution of the day mitigated strongly against it. His Aunt/Mother Prajapatti eventually got him to relent and was the first ordained Bikkhuni.

Bodhi - Awakening or enlightenment.

Bodhi Tree - The tree the Buddha sat under when he attained enlightenment.

Bhodicitta - The body of love and compassion that one draws upon to live as a boddhisattva.

Boddhisattva - This is a person who lives a life dedicated to becoming a Buddha and lives to liberate all sentient beings. During the course of the Jataka stories, the Buddha develops the ten perfections as a Boddhisattva through many lives.

Buddha - Awakened One. Buddha is a title and not a name. Everyone will become a Buddha.

Buddha Nature - The essence of the Buddha, which lies at the heart of all beings. It is the one thing that is seen to be uncreated, unborn and therefore undying. It is as close as the Buddha ever came to describing an actual self in all beings. The qualities of compassion, love, and one-ness are seen to be qualities of Buddha Nature.

Buddhism - The religion based upon the teachings of the Shakyamuni Buddha or most recent manifestation of the Buddha in the world. There is some debate over whether or not Buddhism is a religion, since in its pure form there is no discussion or concept of a deity or worship. At the core of Buddhism is the ideal of freedom from suffering and the attainment of enlightenment. It can also be argued that the idea of Buddha Nature is actually a concept of God. Buddhism is 2,600 years old and originated in Nepal.

Dalai Lama - Literally "Big Sea Guru"- Is both the religious head of Tibetan Buddhism and head of State for Tibet, currently in exile. Believed to be constantly reincarnating Boddhisattva of Compassion, Avalokiteśvara.

Deva - a benevolent supernatural being.

Dharma - The truth or reality that forms the foundation of everything as well as the manifestations of that reality.

Dharmapada - A collection of Buddhist thought in verse form said to have been from the words of the Buddha.

Dukkha - Suffering, dissatisfaction. The actual word the Buddha used when talking about suffering. Its meaning is more multi-dimensional than the English word suffering.

Four Noble Truths - 1. Suffering exists, 2. There is a cause of Suffering, 3. Suffering can be ended, and 4. There's a path out of suffering. This is the first lesson the Buddha ever taught as the Buddha and is the central tenet of Buddhism.

Gasho - palms up and together in a prayerful manner accompanied by a small bow is a respectful way to say thank you.

Gautama Buddha - Yet another name for the most recent Buddha born 2,600 years ago.

Jataka Tales - Collection of 527 stories attributed to the Buddha referring to the past lives he experienced in his journey from Boddhisattva to Buddha.

Kinhin - Walking Meditation.

Koan - A puzzle or story that can only be understood through meditation and direct experience, not by rational thought. Used by teachers to train students in the ways of Zen. Example: What is the sound of one hand clapping?

Lama - A Tibetan Master.

Lineage - In Zen Buddhist practice, the Dharma can only be transmitted from Master to student. Your lineage traces back the ancestry of your Master's Masters. Once you become a Master you are said to be of that lineage. There are Dharma brothers and sisters (those who learned from your same Master.)

Mahayana - "Great Vehicle" is a major branch of Buddhism. Pure Land and Tibetan Buddhism are two of its major sects.

Maitreya - Future Buddha. Most recognizable form as fat jolly monk many people are familiar with and mistakenly think of as the Buddha.

Makyo - Irrelevant thoughts, distractions and experiences during meditation. Psychic phenomenon falls into this category.

Mantra - Chant used as a focal point in some forms of meditation.

Metta - Loving Kindness

Middle Way - Buddhism is called the Middle Way because the Buddha came to realize that extremes of any kind are unhelpful in attaining freedom. He used the analogy of the lute string, which if it is too loose will make no sound and if it is too tight will break. Optimal tuning is in the middle.

Mindfulness - The practice of being fully aware of everything in every moment as it occurs both internally and externally. It is synonymous with "being awake."

Mudra - Positions of the hands during meditation.

Nirvana - The joyous state one enters when they have attained freedom from suffering and are truly awake.

Noble Eightfold Path - The prescription for how to end suffering and the fourth Noble Truth. The eight are: 1.Right View, 2.Right Thought, 3.Right Speech, 4.Right Action, 5.Right Living, 6.Right Effort, 7.Right Mindfulness, and 8.Right Concentration.

Pure Land Buddhism - In a time before Shakyamuni, a preceding Buddha was a monk named Dharmakara who made a vow that, on his attaining Buddhahood, all who had faith in him and who called upon his name would be reborn in his paradise and would reside there in bliss until they had attained enlightenment. This Buddha is called Amitabha and the place is called the Pure Land. This is a Mahayana sect popular in much of eastern Asia.

Reincarnation and Rebirth - The process whereby one goes through many lives in many forms.

Refuge - See; Three Jewels "I take refuge in the Buddha, the Dharma and the Sangha."

Rinpoche - Honorific applied to Tibetan monks who have been recognized as reincarnated masters.

Rinzai - Zen sect that uses Koans.

Roshi - Honorific meaning teacher or Master.

Samsara - The cycle of rebirth.

Sangha - A community of fellow practitioners, monastery.

Satori - Awakening.

Sesshin - Zen intensive retreat that lasts for a matter of days or more.

Shakyamuni Buddha - see Gautama Buddha.

Soto - Zen sect focused on meditation.

Sutra - Scripture.

Tathagata - A term the Buddha used to refer to himself which translates as "Thus Gone" meant to imply this is someone who has completed his journey and has "been there."

Theravada - "Words of the Elders" Major branch of Buddhism. The oldest surviving school of Buddhism incorporates the idea that enlightenment is immediate when it happens, not gradual, Vipassana is a form of Theravadan Buddhism.

Thich - Title used to identify Vietnamese monks.

Three Jewels - Buddha, Dharma, Sangha, (Teacher, Teachings, Community), the three places one can take refuge in. **also** see **Refuge.**

Three Poisons - Clinging, Avoidance, Ignorance. The three major causes of suffering.

Vipassana Meditation - Insight Meditation. Very popular in the U.S. currently.

Zazen - Zen form of sitting meditation.

Zen - Zen emphasizes the attainment of enlightenment and the personal expression of direct insight in the Buddhist teachings. As such, it de-emphasizes mere knowledge of sutras and doctrine and favors direct understanding through zazen and interaction with an accomplished teacher. Literal: meditation.

Zendo - Place where zazen is practiced.

INDEX

CONNECT WITH THE AUTHOR

Website:	www.MeetTheBuddha.com
Email:	MarshallStern@gmail.com
FaceBook:	facebook.com/meetthebuddha
Twitter:	@marshallzen
Zenprov Podcast:	cia.libsyn.com or search iTunes
Online Courses:	Zen Buddhism 101 - Udemy.com

Marshall is available for hire to speak, teach workshops on Zen, Joyful Living and as a consultant on Applying Zen Principles to Optimize your Business.

Marshall is also a Life Coach. Please contact him if you would like him to work with you to awaken your natural joy!

Made in the USA
San Bernardino, CA
23 October 2018